Everyday Cooking for Beginners
BREAK THAT KITCHEN IN!

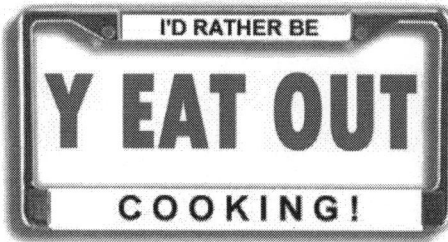

I'D RATHER BE

Y EAT OUT

C O O K I N G !

by
Vineeth Subramanyam

Everyday Cooking for Beginners: Break that kitchen in!
by Vineeth Subramanyam

Front cover:

- Flambe photo courtesy of Linda Stradley and her website *What's Cooking America* at http://whatscookingamerica.net/
- Veggies photo courtesy of Vinu Yamunan. For more details about Vinu's work or to contact him, visit http://www.yvinu.com/

QUESTIONS or COMMENTS?
Write to the author at EverydayCooking@gmail.com
Visit the author's website at http://www.vineeths.com/

DISCLAIMER
The content and recipes presented in this book are a collection of my ideas and what I have learned largely through experimentation. To the best of my knowledge, I have cited references as appropriate and presented the material accurately. However, I wish to remind readers of this book that the process of cooking requires great care – safety, hygiene and sound sense in particular are prerequisites. As a result, I cannot be held responsible for accidents of any kind including but not limited to bodily injury, food poisoning, fires, etc. that may result from following the ideas in this book. Many of the claims made in this book including but not limited to the monetary and health benefits of cooking represent what I have personally observed – individual results may vary. The purpose of this book is to present the reader with an introduction to everyday cooking and encourage readers to build on this knowledge and eventually create their own ideas.

To my parents, the greatest cooks I've ever known

Acknowledgements

THIS BOOK WOULD have been a passing thought but for the continuous support of friends & family. Thanks to those who reviewed the content and provided useful feedback. Thanks to the authors of books and articles that I was able to use as references to complete my work. Thanks to the motley crowd of Chefs on and off television who have helped me take a bigger bite out of life. Finally, thanks to everyone who believed in me, encouraged me and showed genuine interest in my project.

Thanks in particular to Olga Draskovic, Vikram Subramanyam, Vidya Guda, Yadu Badarayan, Sindhu Satish and Jyothsna Kumaraswamy. Special thanks to Pamela Metivier, Satyajeet Salgar, Dale Cook, Brijesh Kurup and Vikram Vuppala for providing feedback on the content and design of the book. Thanks to Vinu Yamunan for shooting the "veggies" cover image and to Linda Stradley for providing the "flambé" cover image. Thanks to Aimee Lloyd for her input on the cover design.

Thanks also to Arjun Parthasarathy, Saverio Spontella, Archil Kublashvili, Catherine Anderson, Mark Christensen, Ben Meisel, Aimee Dawson and many others for sharing my interest in writing this book and their inevitable help in promoting this book.

CONTENTS

Introduction

MY FRIENDS JACK & JILL would buy pre-packaged

boiled water if they could. That pretty much sums up their fondness
for the kitchen. They don't like any of it – the chopping, the
handling, the frying, the sautéing, the baking, the boiling, the
steaming or the cleanup – they'd rather just be eating! On the few
occasions that they have forced themselves into the kitchen, they
have only gotten disheartened and angry for the terrible way they
wasted their time.

We all have friends like Jack and Jill, and many of us *are* Jacks
and Jills. Some of us have asked the question that lingers supreme
in the minds of most kitchen-averse people: *Why cook when I can eat
out?* Well, I love eating out too, but what I hope to do in the

following chapters is to get you thinking about the alternative. Whether you're a beginner, a cooking enthusiast or just flirting with the idea of cooking, this book will help you fend off your reservations, provide a step-by-step readable guide to cooking, offer new ways to appreciate this king of hobbies and add to your collection of recipes. When you're done with this book, you will not look at cooking as a chore any more.

This book has a no nonsense approach in teaching you exactly what you need to know to get started with cooking. The chapters in this book have been written with a beginner in mind, and strive to address all aspects of the cooking process from shopping for groceries, pots and pans to the actual mechanics of cooking and presentation of various dishes. Each chapter also contains a list of takeaways at the end. The book also includes a variety of recipes that have been arranged and labeled for quick retrieval. Here's how each chapter flavors the pot:

Part I

Chapter 1, *Why cook?*, answers the burning question that almost every novice cook has. Quite simply, this chapter lays the foundation for the rest of the book by diving right into the question and providing seven compelling reasons for you to start cooking today. The chapter also provides a roadmap for the rest of the book.

Chapter 2, *Before you cook I: Kitchen,* provides relief for a common source of anxiety for novice cooks. The goal of this chapter is to identify the basic components of a functional kitchen for the beginner and provide a cost estimate for each item. This chapter will be of most help to a beginner who has never set foot in the cooking section of supermarkets.

Chapter 3, *Before you cook II: Groceries,* explores another common source of anxiety of many novice cooks. This chapter starts with a discussion about grocery visits and the ten reasons that people typically overspend at grocery stores. The chapter then provides tangible ways to save on your grocery bills and ends with a discussion on planning grocery visits. If you have ever been unsure about shopping for ingredients at grocery stores, looking for ways to save money or better plan your grocery trips, this chapter is for you!

Chapter 4, *Let's get cooking,* explains the actual cooking process with the beginner in mind. The chapter starts with a discussion of common cooking problems and talks about the three stages of cooking that work for almost every dish: prepping, cooking and assembly. The chapter explains each stage in depth and ends with a discussion of common beginner mistakes. Most of the recipes presented later in Part II of this book follow the guidelines provided in this chapter.

Part II

Chapter 5, *Recipes*, is a collection of the recipes that I've grown to love over the years. Most of them have Indian, Asian and European influences. Each recipe is complete with a detailed list of ingredients, cooking instructions, and serving suggestions. The type of cookware used to prepare each dish is also noted. The recipes directly draw on many of the ideas presented in Part I of this book. The book also contains a glossary of cooking terms, ingredients and spices.

I recommend reading the book in the order written for beginners and cooking enthusiasts alike. The chapters in Part I of the book will introduce you to the world of cooking and dispel your myths, fears and anxieties about the cooking process as a whole. I recommend reading Part I of the book in one sitting. Part II of the book is a collection of recipes and is intended to serve as a resource when you want to cook. You'll find the recipes in this section to be descriptive and easy to follow. As you read through and try these recipes, please keep in mind that the collection of recipes presented here is merely meant to whet your appetite (literally!). After reading through this book and trying the recipes provided here, my hope is that you will experiment with new ingredients, new cuisines and new styles to come up with interesting variations and completely new recipes that you can call your own.

Enjoy the ride!

Vin

Vineeth Subramanyam

EverydayCooking@gmail.com

http://www.vineeths.com/

August 2006

Part I
The Classroom

Why cook?

IT'S 12:00 NOON and you feel that familiar lunch-time

growl in your stomach. You reach for your wallet and head to the

neighborhood lunch spot. Thirty minutes later, you leave satisfied

with a lighter wallet and a quieter stomach. Wait until dinner time,

rinse and repeat. That's the routine for a large portion of the US

population. Until a few years ago, I followed this routine religiously.

It was so convenient and the pre-assigned combo #s only made it

simpler. "I'd like a #3 please", I would say, handing a punch card to

the lady to record my purchase. A few minutes later, my meal would

arrive neatly packaged with a side of fried potatoes and my favorite

beverage to complement. I would sit down, open the package,

devour the treat, wash it down with the sugary drink and head to the trash can to dispose of the empty wrappers. Stepping out on the street, I'd triumphantly glance at the punch card and smile – only four more meals to buy before that coveted free meal.

Three months and five *free* meals later, I started to notice something else – my growing gut and my unimpressive bank balance (I was on a student budget after all). I was also getting tired of toggling between the same choices – combos #1, #3 and #7 – my favorites. I wanted variety. I wanted to eat healthier. I wanted to spend less. As I look back, those were the three biggest motivators for me to start cooking. Over the years, I've added more reasons to that list. In the next few pages, I'll describe seven compelling reasons for you to start cooking today.

7 reasons why you should be cooking

#1: It's healthier

There's no question about it. Cooking your own food is a healthier way to eat. If you've seen the movie *Road Trip*, you might recall the scene from the diner where the boys sit down for breakfast. Suffice it to say, one of the reasons that makes cooking a healthier alternative is that you know exactly what goes into your food. Restaurants sometimes focus largely on only the taste appeal of their menus for better ratings and greater repeat business. This provides a large incentive for restaurants to over-indulge in ingredients that provide taste but little incremental nutrition – like oil, cheese, butter, etc. When you cook, *you* decide what and how much of each ingredient goes into your dish. This moderation, when done right, leads to healthier eating.

#2: It's cheaper

So, how much do you spend on eating out every month? You've probably not really thought about it, but indulge me a little. If you're an average professional who eats out 5 days a week for lunch at $8-$10 and dinner at $12-$16, you're spending about $125 a week or $500 a month. What if I said that you could cut that spending to less than half if you cooked at home? At over $250 a month, that's a savings of about $3,000 a year!

#3: It's your menu

Has this ever happened to you: You're browsing through a restaurant's menu and notice an entrée that looks promising – the right ingredients, the right price, just what you wanted! – you order it and take a bite, only to be disappointed. For the rest of the meal, you're staring at a plate of something you don't want, and the best you can do is offer someone else a taste hoping they'll return favor. Eating out in some sense is like driving a car with automatic transmission: predictable and easy, but without the excitement of hearing the engine roar, begging to be shifted to a different level of performance. Cooking, on the other hand, puts you in the driver's seat. You decide what goes into your dish, the cooking method, the level of spiciness, the texture, whatever – it's your menu!

#4: It's a sense of accomplishment

One of my favorite scenes in the movie *Cast Away* is when Tom Hanks's character proudly proclaims "Look at what I have created!" after starting a fire from scratch. Regardless of what anyone has accomplished in life, it is the fundamental things that often evoke the strongest emotions. Eating is so fundamental, so essential for survival, that creating a plate of good tasting food from inedible raw ingredients provides a sense of accomplishment and independence like no other! It is not a stretch when I say that this independence will actually transfer to other parts of your life and make you a more confident, self-reliant person. Try it to believe it!

#5: It's creative

One of my most memorable moments with cooking happened several years ago when I was in graduate school. I had woken up around 1pm, nursing a hangover and absolutely ravenous. I reached for the fridge, only to find a small bowl of leftover plain rice and an egg – not an appealing combination by any means! In the background, I heard the nasty whistling of a windy snowstorm. A store run was out of question. That day, I cooked fried rice for the first time, using the leftover rice, frozen peas, the egg, some garlic and soy sauce. The result was surprisingly satisfying, and not just because I was hungry. Since then, I've stretched myself to create new recipe ideas with whatever's in the fridge. A few months into this hobby and you too, will learn to make lemonade from lemons, literally!

#6: It's expressive

For many people, self-expression takes the form of the clothes they wear, the cars they drive or even the drinks they get at a bar. Believe it or not, cooking offers a deliciously different form of self-expression. In the recipe section of this book, I share some recipes that were inspired from my travels (fusion recipes like *crepes stuffed with kheema*) and others that are new twists on traditional recipes. In fact, every step of cooking, from chopping ingredients to presenting the final product provides an opportunity for self-expression. As you read through the book and become familiar with the cooking process, I encourage you to put your recipes in the context of your own experiences to create new ways to express yourself.

#7: It's cool

Cooking has never been more popular. More Americans are tuning in to cooking shows than ever before. Our love for food has propelled the Food Network, which started as recently as 1993, to one of the fastest growing networks on television. Trust me when I say that you'll instantly impress people by simply mentioning that you can cook. You'll make lasting friends by throwing dinner parties. If you are a single guy, more girls will notice you, guaranteed! As you continue to indulge in this hobby, you'll get to know food better, order like a pro at restaurants, and even pair wine with your food easily. You'll eat healthier, spend less, feel more confident and experience a freedom unlike any other. Heck, you'll even make your mama proud.

Ok, I want to cook – what next?

The chapters in this book have been carefully written to cover every aspect of concern that a beginner cook usually has. The next two chapters will specifically address what you need to take care of before you start cooking. Chapter 2 will take you through a step-by-step process to set up your basic kitchen. Chapter 3 will walk you through the seemingly mysterious aisles of the grocery store, with several money-saving tips, to help you shop for the right ingredients before you begin cooking. Chapter 4 will teach you the mechanics of cooking through three stages – the prepping of ingredients, the actual cooking process and the presentation. You'll learn how to break up your cooking into steps that add flavor, variety, texture, etc. Finally, Part II of this book will provide forty sample recipes with detailed instruction steps that you can immediately try at home. Let's get started shall we?

Chapter 1 Takeaways

The 7 reasons why you should be cooking:
- Cooking is a healthier alternative
- Cooking can potentially save you $3,000 a year
- Cooking gives you control to create what **you** want
- Cooking leaves you with a sense of accomplishment and increased confidence
- Cooking draws out your creative side
- Cooking is a great way to express yourself
- Cooking is cool!

Before you cook I: Kitchen

ONE OF THE BIGGEST sources of anxiety for novice

cooks is the process of setting up their kitchen. What kind of pots

and pans should I get? What about cookware – is a wok better than

a skillet? Is it necessary to get a saucepan? If so, what size? In many

respects, shopping for cookware is like shopping for a new

wardrobe – and if you're not careful, may end up costing as much.

Much like you need clothes for every season, so do you need a

different piece of cookware for different styles of cooking. The

criteria remain the same: function, durability, style, price and

comfort (yes, comfort). And as with clothes, you pay a pretty

penny for name brands.

The list below provides a basic list of must-haves for your kitchen. This list is all you should need to prep, cook and present your dish.

9 elements of a basic kitchen

#1: Chopping Block

This is where it all begins. Look for a surface that is gentle on your knives and gentle on your ears (yes, some chopping boards are noisy). Trust me, the last thing you need is an uneven surface when dealing with sharp edges. I've found that sturdy wooden "butcher" blocks are perfect for the job. The weight of the block keeps it from moving; the wood is gentle against the knife; and the cutting has a smooth dull feel, and an unobtrusive sound. So if you have one of those thin glass cutting-boards, double it as a serving plate and invest in a wooden block instead. Among the other benefits, a good chopping experience is a great set up for the remainder of the cooking process. [Cost: $10-$25]

#2: Knives & Spatulas

You'll be surprised at how expensive a set of knives can be - you could buy a small television for the same price. Consider your cooking needs before investing in a fancy set of knives. Are you a vegetarian? Are you a barbeque enthusiast? Do you eat a lot of fish? This will help you decide if you need a set of steak knives for the dinner table, special knives for fish or a simple all-purpose Chef's knife. For the purposes of home cooking, a single Chef's knife, a bread knife and a smaller flexible knife will meet almost every chopping need in the kitchen. One of the best ways to get started is to invest in an inexpensive knife set – mine has 1 Chef's knife, 1 bread knife, 1 paring knife, 6 steak knives, a whisk, couple of spatulas, all for under $30. [Cost: $30-$40]

#3: Whisk

Most people associate a whisk with beating eggs, but the whisk is more versatile than you'd think. A whisk not only mixes ingredients together, but it also provides a way to incorporate air into the ingredients. This especially comes in handy when mixing light batters for crepes, pancakes, or the like; or for mixing eggs for a fluffy omelet. Mixing with a whisk is also amazingly effective at getting rid of lumps in batters without the need for buying expensive powered mixers. [Cost: $10]

#4: Salad/all-purpose bowls

Salad bowls get a lot of use in the kitchen, even if not used specifically for salads. These bowls are perfect for marinating meats, mixing batters or for storing leftovers. The bowls are also great for mixing fruits, nuts and honey to create invigorating fruit salads. In the recipe section, you'll find several recipes for crepes, fruit salads, omelets and many other dishes that specifically call for mixing in these bowls. The versatility of these bowls makes them a must-have in the kitchen. A set of three bowls is usually sufficient. [Cost: $20-$30]

#5: Wok

The wok is probably the most versatile piece of cookware in a kitchen. And that makes it my personal favorite tool in the kitchen – I repeatedly reach for it to cook almost any dish. A wok is a round-bottomed pan that conveniently collects oil at the base for easy frying. The utensil is most often used for stir-frying, shallow-frying, deep-frying, boiling, steaming, poaching, and many other styles of cooking. [Cost: $20-$30]

#6: 12" sauté pan

A sauté pan is a must-have for cooking any dish that requires even heat over a wide surface area. Examples of dishes you'll cook with a sauté pan include omelets, scrambled eggs, crepes and several one-pan dishes. It is important to buy a sauté pan that comes with a lid. [Cost: $20-$30]

#7: Saucepans/stockpots

While a wok will suffice for most cooking needs, it falls short for dishes that need to contain large amounts of liquid – e.g., soups, chili, stews, gravies, or for heating stock or milk. For such uses, saucepans usually work best. Saucepans are also great for Indian dishes like *sambar* and *rasam*. Saucepans come in different sizes, but generally a 3-quart or 5-quart saucepan should work well for most recipes. [Cost: $40]

#8: Casserole dish

For the longest time, I used to cook rice on the stove, just like every thing else. But for sometime now, I have been using a casserole dish to cook rice in the microwave. A casserole dish is obviously good for making casseroles, but is also good for making dishes that call for baking. Casserole dishes also double as good serving dishes for the finished product. You'll definitely want to keep one in your kitchen. [Cost: $20]

#9: Bake ware

So when was the last time you put anything in the oven? When I think of baking, I flash back to the day when I was cleaning my grad school apartment in Columbia, Missouri before leaving for Chicago for my first job. Cleaning a messy apartment was a tough chore, but there was one place I didn't have to worry about – the oven. Even though I had been cooking regularly for about a year through grad school, I had never been bold enough to use the oven. As I've gotten into cooking over the years, the oven now plays an important role in my culinary escapades. Having some pieces of bake ware is essential to any kitchen – a cookie sheet and a deep dish (round or square) at the minimum will serve you well even if you just eat a lot of frozen pizzas! [Cost: $20-$30]

And that's it! The above items should set you up with a basic functional kitchen, at a combined cost of around $200-$250. If you shop around, you could potentially cut the cost to about $150. This measly set up cost could now help you save over $3,000 during the first year alone! Now that you have a functional kitchen, let's talk about the next important step: shopping for groceries.

Chapter 2 Takeaways

The 9 things you need to set up a basic functional kitchen:

- Chopping block [$10-$20]
- Knives & Spatulas [$30-$40]
- Whisk [$10]
- Salad/all-purpose bowls [$20-$30]
- Wok [$20-$30]
- 12" sauté pan [$20-$30]
- Saucepans/stockpots [$40]
- Casserole dish [$20]
- Bake ware [$20-$30]

For a total cost of $200-$250 (or $150 if you shop around), you could be saving $3,000 a year by cooking at home!

3

Before you cook II: Groceries

THE FIRST TIME I walked into a grocery store in the US

was several years ago, when I had spent barely a week in the
country having just flown in from India. Let's just say that I was
pleasantly overwhelmed. The choice was incredible. There were at
least ten varieties of everything – chips, crackers, breakfast cereal,
chocolate, you name it. Each package had colorful pictures and
descriptive phrases that screamed: "You want me". There were all
kinds of meats. There was something for every cook from frozen
dinners to goat cheese. There were even pre-cut vegetables. A food
lover's paradise! I was home.

Three hours passed by before I marched out the exit door with six full bags worth $100. Then, I suddenly stopped when I realized that I didn't have a car – I had actually walked over with a friend, with the intention of buying toothpaste. *How did I spend $100?!* Five seconds later, my friend emerged from the exit as well. His damage was $150. We were lucky to hitch a ride home that day. Walking home with thirteen full bags between the two of us would have been ugly.

That was several years ago. I look back on those days with a smile – a sign of grocery-shopping maturity, if you will. I now understand why I spent more time and money buying things I probably never used. Today, my grocery shopping lasts 10-15 minutes including the wait at the checkout line. If I go in for toothpaste, I come out with toothpaste and nothing else.

10 ways to control grocery spending

The grocery shopping business is a $500+ billion industry in the US, not too far behind the electronics industry. Apples and oranges, you may say – after all, a $20 grocery bill pales in comparison to a $700 camcorder bill. But tally your own grocery bills for the year and you may be surprised at what you find. Not all the money spent in grocery stores is on food. And not all the food we buy from grocery stores is consumed. We've all seen the strawberries rot, the milk cartons go past their expiration date and the veggies become soggy. I'm yet to see a refrigerator that didn't have something trash-worthy. Americans shop at grocery stores once a week on average, but throw away a portion of their grocery expenditure in the trash every year. With a monthly bill of $300 and 15% wastage, that's $540 in the trash every year. That money could buy a home entertainment system. In most cases, our buying habits are to blame for this wastage, and can fortunately be corrected.

Broadly speaking, we buy two kinds of products: those we *need* and those we *want*. Basic necessities like toothpaste and toilet paper are products we use everyday. Such commodity products are typically inexpensive. On the other hand, the latest DVD player or car is not something we need for survival, but rather something we want. Such products tend to be more expensive, and are bought only a few times during our lives. Food is an intriguing amalgam of the two product types. We *need* food for survival, and at the same time, we don't just *want* food, we *crave* it[1]. The problem of grocery shopping is fueled by more than just the enticing displays in the aisles. There are at least ten factors that influence our expenditure, but in our control:

#1: Resist impulse purchases

Impulse purchase refers to unintentional purchases that were not originally on a shopping list. In fact, research has shown that more than two-thirds of our buying decisions are made after we enter the grocery store. Impulse buying decisions typically make up 20%-50% of a typical grocery bill. You might have noticed that convenience

---

[1] According to a survey conducted in the UK, 59% of the women surveyed said that they preferred food to sex [see references]

items like milk, eggs and yogurt are usually placed in the back of grocery stores – a customer has to walk through scores of goodies in the aisles to get there. There's plenty of opportunity to stray from a pre-defined shopping list. Ask yourself how many times you have bought something at the checkout counter, and whether it was on your original list.

#2: Avoid unnecessary purchases

How many times have you bought milk at the grocery store only to see an extra gallon of milk waiting at home? The same happens with yogurt, cheese, strawberries, herbs, etc. It is always best to peek inside your refrigerator, pantry and kitchen before heading out to the grocery store. You don't want to buy something you don't need.

#3: Be careful about bulk shopping

People often buy in bulk to save money, but it doesn't always turn out that way. Be sure to look at the expiration date. It hurts to throw away a gallon of chocolate milk that expired before the urge for a second cup. Also, shopping for groceries in small quantities when you need them gives you the freshest ingredients to cook with. The next section in this chapter will describe how you can better plan your visits to the grocery store.

#4: Don't shop hungry

Believe it or not, research has shown that the hungrier we are, the more we spend at grocery stores. So the next time you're really hungry and want to run to the grocery store, drink a tall glass of water before you enter. The water will help curb your hunger and retain more dollars in your pocket.

#5: Look for expiration dates

Many people don't pay attention to expiration dates on products like dairy, eggs and juice. You always want to buy products that will stay fresh longer, so when looking at expiration dates, always reach behind what you see up front. The milk cartons displayed in the front row almost always have a closer expiration date than the ones behind. Getting a product that has been marked to expire further out will give you more time to use it.

#6: Pay attention to the unit of sale

People often don't pay attention to the unit of sale at grocery stores: is the price per item, per bag or per pound? Needless to say, if the unit of sale is an individual item, you'll maximize your value by picking up the largest item you can find. Also, when buying packaged food in bulk, you'll maximize your value by choosing the item that costs the least per pound. It is important to pay attention to units when shopping for groceries!

#7: Don't pay for unnecessary labor

Grocery stores often offer customers a choice of vegetables in their natural form or pre-cut vegetables. Along the same lines, there are pre-arranged fruit platters and party veggie platters. You can save a bundle by buying the ingredients in their natural form and doing the cutting yourself.

#8: Take advantage of store discounts

Many stores have private label products that are sometimes as good as the bigger brands. Try the store brands! Also, take advantage of the loyalty cards at grocery stores and plan to shop at the same store week after week. You'll be amazed at how much you'll save.

#9: Walk to the grocery store

Walk to the grocery store if possible. The absence of a car will force you to buy in smaller quantities – if you have a shopping list, you'll tend to stick to it. Even if you stray from the list, you'll be forced to make intelligent decisions to make it easy to walk back home.

#10: Use cash for quick runs

Leave the credit card at home when shopping for small items like toothpaste. If you can't pay, you can't stray!

What and how much to buy?

Now that you know how to shop wisely, let's talk about what and how much of an item you should buy. In many respects, shopping for groceries is like inventory management – you buy certain quantities, store it in your fridge where you pay a holding cost (if your groceries go bad) and at the end of one period, whatever that is, you're ready to order again. What makes grocery shopping challenging sometimes is that most items are perishable, but with different expiration patterns. Fortunately, you don't need the latest inventory management software to give you optimal quantities and lead times for your orders.

Effective grocery shopping comes down to having an idea of two things for each item on your shopping list: your consumption pattern and the expiration date of the item. When expiration dates are not marked (e.g., vegetables, fruits, herbs, etc.), try to buy enough to last you for a week only. When expiration dates are given, do a quick check with your consumption pattern. For example, say you consume an 8oz glass of milk every morning. At this rate, a half-gallon (64oz) carton of milk will last you for 8 days. So given a choice between a half-gallon carton that expires in 10 days and a gallon that expires in 10 days, you would pick the half-gallon carton, even if you're paying a higher unit cost. On the other hand, if you have a domestic partner or roommate who also has a similar consumption pattern, you want to get the full gallon of milk. As a rule of thumb, when you're considering any item in the store, start with your consumption pattern to get an idea for how soon you will consume the entire product. Then, make sure the product is going to stay fresh at least until that date.

The frequency of your visits to the grocery store will depend on your proximity to the store. If you live right next to a grocery store, buy enough to last you for 2-3 days (you can always go back if you need to). If you live further away, shop for a week's worth of groceries. The trick is to keep your items as fresh as you can. I find that a weekly visit to the grocery store is the most effective way to shop for my consumption pattern – you should find your own.

If you're new to grocery shopping, the chart at the end of this chapter will serve you well in the grocery store. The chart breaks down the grocery shopping process into two steps: (1) What you must do *before* entering the grocery store and (2) What you must do *inside* the grocery store. The chart draws on the ideas presented in this chapter that will help you plan your grocery visits according to your consumption pattern and save you time and money. In particular, the chart provides different approaches for perishable items (those that will expire before a reasonable length of time) and non-perishable items (those that can be reasonably expected to stay fresh until consumed). Apply this technique for a couple of weeks and soon, you'll be shopping like a pro without even thinking about it.

A note on online grocers

Although majority of us shop for groceries once a week, a large number of us (60%) don't really like the experience[2]! Online grocers are a boon to those who hate wheeling the cart. More people have embraced e-tailing than ever before. Online stores generally succeed if they offer a more convenient service that saves money. People are

---

[2] Grocery shopping is a $500B/year market in the US, 60% of consumers dislike grocery shopping [see references]

also inclined to buy online if they hate shopping at brick-and-mortar stores – as is the case for prescription drugs (who has ever enjoyed a trip to the pharmacy to get medicine?). But the idea of selling groceries online has been debated endlessly.

Shopping for your weekly supplies online has its advantages of course: there is no waiting at a checkout line, no wobbly cart to train your muscles, and no time wasted walking any aisles. Online grocers also remember previous purchases, making it fast and easy to re-order. A big advantage of shopping online is that it reduces the tendency to buy on impulse; and eliminates at least half the over-spending risks mentioned above. At the same time, some argue that grocery shopping is not something that can be delegated to a machine. Online stores simply don't provide the human aspect of shopping, which is important for grocery shopping (if you figure out a way to squeeze fruit on a web page, I'd love to know). Further, shoppers don't like the waiting and planning involved for taking delivery of their groceries. Like other e-tailers, online grocers also have to battle the instant turn-off of shipping charges: customers don't like them!

I embraced online shopping a long time ago, but food is one of two products I couldn't buy online[3]. I'm in the second camp that wants to inspect their groceries before buying. You have to make the decision for yourself, of course. But with the inevitable hungry stomach that wants instant gratification, chances are you won't escape the real thing.

---

[3] Clothing is the other.

GROCERY SHOPPING CHART

BEFORE LEAVING HOME

Make a list of items you need (the list below is a starting point). Peek in your fridge to note which items are running low and how long they'll last:

- **Breakfast foods:** Milk, Cereal, Eggs, Bread, Butter, Jam, Coffee
- **Meal time foods:** Vegetables, Meat, Fish, Herbs, Spices
- **Desserts:** Fruits, Nuts, Honey, Ice cream, Cake
- **Snack food:** Chips, Salsa, Cookies

INSIDE THE GROCERY STORE

Once inside the grocery store, visit ONLY the aisles that contain the items on your list (just go top-down from breakfast foods to snack foods). As you go through your list, make sure each item passes this general test before you place it in your shopping cart:

If item is **NOT perishable** (e.g., cereal, coffee, paper towels)
  → Find the best **unit price** (bulk sizes are cheaper)
    → PLACE ITEM IN THE CART

If item is **perishable** (e.g., dairy, vegetables, fruits)
    → Find all sizes that you can consume before next grocery visit
      → Only consider sizes that will stay fresh until next visit
        → Find the best **unit price** on largest size
          → PLACE ITEM IN THE CART

Chapter 3 Takeaways

The 10 ways to control grocery spending:
- Resist impulse purchases
- Avoid unnecessary purchases (peek in your fridge before going to the grocery store)
- Be careful about bulk shopping
- Don't shop hungry
- Look for expiration dates
- Pay attention to the unit of sale
- Don't pay for unnecessary labor
- Take advantage of store discounts
- Walk to the grocery store
- Use cash for quick runs

What and how much to buy?
- What is your consumption pattern?
- How soon will this product expire?
- Bottom line: If you can't consume the item before it perishes, don't buy!

4
Let's get cooking!

THE KITCHEN IS one of those places where mathematical axioms don't necessarily make sense. In this world, two plus two is definitely not equal to four. Cooking would probably never have developed as it has today if we were all content with eating individual foods separately. Indeed, one of the most interesting aspects of cooking is combining ingredients that go well together, such that eating them together is more satisfying than eating each ingredient individually. Like anything else, practice makes perfect in the kitchen. And sometimes, there's just no better feeling than coming back to your kitchen with a bag of fresh groceries that promise endless combinations for the trying. Well, pour yourself a glass of good wine and read along – you might just learn something new!

The 3 stages of cooking

On a high level, there are three stages to serving any dish: prepping the ingredients, cooking, and assembling them – all of which merit due attention. In the sections below, I will describe each of these stages in detail.

Stage #1: Prepping your food

People who are new to cooking seldom pay attention to this all-important step; they are eager to get to the cooking stage. Jumping right into cooking without the required pre-work is like painting a wall without the first coat of primer, or exercising without warming-up. In fact, everything that happens during the cooking stage depends on the outcome of the prep stage. The following prep methods are most common:

Identify all ingredients

Before you begin cooking, spend a few minutes to identify all ingredients that will go into your dish. In particular, break down the dish into three parts: the flavor, the body and the garnish. In other words, what are the set of ingredients that will flavor your dish? Example ingredients of this type could be garlic, ginger, assorted spices, herbs, etc. Next, what are the set of ingredients that will make the body of your dish – this is essentially what the dish is about. Example ingredients of this type would be assorted meats and vegetables. Finally, what kind of garnish is appropriate for this dish? Examples of this type include assorted nuts, herbs or pan sauces (more on this later).

Chopping

Chopping ingredients is involved in almost every dish, but it is especially important for a stir-fry, or any dish that is cooked on high heat in a short amount of time. For cooking such dishes, it may be essential to have an assortment of chopped ingredients readily available so as to not slow down the cooking process. The ingredients are often added in a pre-defined order, and there's little time to chop & cook simultaneously! If chopping is deferred to the cooking stage, there's a risk of overcooking or burning the ingredients in the flaming wok. Same goes for dishes like scrambled eggs (recipe included in this book). In fact, crafting a plan for cooking your dish starts with chopping of ingredients – should the ingredients be minced, diced or left in chunks? It is customary to use a rough chop on the main ingredient of the dish and a fine chop on accompanying ingredients that serve to bring out the flavor of the main ingredient.

Marinating

Marinating is another way of prepping food, before cooking actually begins. If you've never heard of the term, marinating is simply a way to enrich the flavor of ingredients by soaking them in a motley assortment of seasonings, juices and sauces. This step is most often followed with meat, chicken or seafood dishes. There are several ways to marinate food: some meats are soaked for less than an hour, some for a few hours, and some overnight or longer. Marinating is a critical step for many dishes because the choice of seasonings and the length of time that the food soaks for largely define the flavor of the dish. A basic rule is that heavier (or denser) meats marinate for longer: so a leg of lamb will usually marinate for 12-24 hours, a chicken breast typically requires 3 hours or less, a fish filet will probably only need a ½ hour's soak. Similarly, the ingredients in a marinade also go from 'light' to 'heavy' depending on the meat. A leg of lamb may soak in a mix of many aromatic seasonings – paprika, cumin, ginger, garlic, salt, pepper, limejuice, herbs, etc. – but a filet of fish may need just a little limejuice and some pepper to wake its flavors up. As you go through the recipes later, you'll find plenty of examples that illustrate this critical step.

Stage #2: Cooking in layers

We've all been there. You're at a friend's house for dinner and you take a bite of the main course. And there's a part of you that is actually offended for being tortured in this way: each morsel is a dreadful surprise. Either the food is undercooked, or bland in some bites and way too salty in some, or worse, you can't really put a finger on it. You control the urge to toss the food in the dumpster, and instead smile and silently suffer for this hostess with no prowess! After attending a few less than appetizing dinners myself, I decided to investigate this all too common fiasco in the kitchen. As my curiosity in cooking began to grow, I asked myself several questions: How do some dishes get unevenly cooked? How do they get unevenly seasoned? What is the right way to cook? Given that most dishes contain an assortment of ingredients, each with different degrees of doneness and cooking times, how can they be made to come together? Is there a "right" method that works every time or at least most of the time?

Fortunately, by flipping through some cooking shows, reading some books and much experimentation, I was able to answer my questions. Regardless of the cooking method, I have found that one of the most effective ways to cook is to work in layers. Cooking in this way offers control over not only how long each ingredient cooks, but also the even distribution of spices throughout the dish. In this sense, cooking is like building a house, which begins with a foundation and each incremental step builds on the previous step.

Build the flavor base

As a common rule, the first step to layering is to identify the background flavors of the dish – these are flavors that can be tasted in every bite. These ingredients are among the first to be added to your dish. Examples of such ingredients are onions, ginger, garlic, tomato paste & selected spices (the *masala*) in most north-Indian recipes, green peppers & celery and onion (the *trinity*) in many Cajun recipes and carrots, celery & onion (the *mirepoix*) in French and American cooking. These background flavors may differ from those used to marinate the main ingredients during the prepping stage.

Add ingredients in a specific order

Having built a flavor base, the next step is to add ingredients in the descending order of their cooking times. For example, if you're making a potato-spinach curry, add potatoes to the flavor base first since they take longer to cook. Pay attention also to the surface area of the different pieces – e.g., a chunky piece of carrot will take more time to cook than a julienne (thin strip) piece. As each ingredient is added, sprinkle a fresh layer of seasoning on top. Allow the ingredients to cook partially before adding the next ingredient. Continue to build these layers of ingredients and flavors until all the ingredients are cooked and all the flavors are absorbed.

Allow the dish to come together

After the dish is mostly cooked, it is important to allow the dish to "come together". What this specifically refers to is different for each dish. For example, if you're cooking a soup, stew or chili, it is important to simmer on low heat for an extended period of time after all the ingredients have been added. If you're making a stir-fry, it is important to spend an additional thirty to sixty seconds tossing the ingredients together on high heat. If you're baking pork tenderloin, it is important to allow it to rest for a few minutes after taking it out of the oven. This is a critical cooking step that allows all the flavors that have been built up thus far to mingle with each other and bring the dish together. Finally, depending on the dish, it may be a good idea to remove the dish into a different container and make a pan sauce with the flavorful bits stuck to the bottom of the pan. A pan sauce is usually a reduction of wine, stock or water that absorbs all the remaining flavors from the pot, and is usually poured right on top of the finished product.

Stage #3: The assembly

Given that eating is such a sensory experience, assembling the final dish for consumption is an important part of the cooking process. Assembling goes beyond visual presentation – it influences our enjoyment of the dish in many ways. As with the cooking stage, the magic of layering persists through this final step of serving the dish. Examine the dishes you eat everyday, and you're likely to notice that almost every dish supports the underlying concept of layering. Steaks are usually topped with a layer of sautéed mushrooms, Indian curries are layered over steamed rice, and Mexican tacos and burritos are essentially layers of cooked food rolled together. Even sushi, which typically contains raw fish, is presented in layers. Foods that don't fall under this umbrella with respect to the dish are presented as side dishes. Layering really works well in presentation because it conforms to the way we eat! The feeling of different ingredients coming together in our mouth gives us the sensation of good taste. Later in this book, you'll find many presentation ideas for the recipes that follow.

A few things to watch out for

The process of cooking requires great care – safety, hygiene and sound sense in particular are prerequisites. In particular, there are three things that are especially common among beginners – call them mistakes, over-indulgence, negligence or whatever:

Heat

"Use your knob!" yells a famous chef on his television show. What he refers to is an all too common problem, especially among beginners. A surprising number of people have an affinity for cooking on high heat. Maybe it is related to the busy lifestyles we lead, that we're in a rush to cook our dishes ASAP. But cooking on high heat for a short time is not the same as simmering on low heat for a long time (another breakdown of mathematical rules). And this rule is all too important to ignore for the sake of rushing. The choice of cooking temperature influences not just the degree of doneness, but also the texture of the ingredients and how they complement each other. It directly influences the look and feel of the dish, and indirectly, the smell of the dish. It is easy to forget how much of an impact the cooking temperature has on our sensory perception of the dish. Every dish has unique requirements for the degree of heat. A pot of chili needs to be simmered on low heat for hours; the goal here is to break down the bonds in the meat to make it tender, and for the meat to absorb the surrounding flavors in the sauce, and to impart its own flavor into the sauce. Crusty pork tenderloin, on the other hand, has to be dusted with flour and seared on high heat to create a crisp texture on the outside that forms a seal, which prevents the juices from running when the tenderloin finishes in the oven. So pay attention to the knobs on your stove – you may just surprise yourself with the results, and keep the smoke alarm from waking up your neighbors.

Spices

"Five stars, and hot sauce on the side" was my standard response to the "how spicy?" question at Asian eateries for the longest time. So it wasn't surprising that I took this bring-it-on philosophy with me to the kitchen when I started cooking. Adding spices to ingredients is a great way to enrich flavor, but when overdone, all dishes could start to taste alike. If the seasonings overshadow the main ingredient in the dish, you may notice that a potato curry, a cauliflower curry and a mushroom curry all exude the same flavor in your mouth. If you're in this camp, do make an effort to back off on the spices a bit – your digestive system will thank you for it, and you might just taste the vegetables and meats you're cooking!

Cleanliness

When it comes to food and cooking, cleanliness is sacrosanct. After all, you're going to be putting that in your mouth! For most people, the nuisance of cleaning up is the sole reason for not choosing to cook in the first place. But it doesn't have to be that way. The three stage cooking process described in this chapter is not only an effective way to divide the cleanup effort but also a critical way to enforce good kitchen hygiene. Before starting the prep stage of cooking (stage #1), I've found it helpful to keep an empty plastic bag to collect all the trash. If the dish calls for meat, I always begin by trimming the fat and chopping the meat into portions. As I go through this process, the trimmed ends and fat go into the plastic bag and the bite size meat portions go into a clean bowl on the side. Next, I thoroughly wash and sanitize the chopping board, knife and my hands (always important when you're dealing with meat). Then I marinate the meat, wash my hands again and begin to cut vegetables, again dropping all the trash in to the plastic bag. At the end of the prep stage, cleanup is as easy as disposing of the plastic bag into the trash can!

Let's dig in!

With that, let's dive into this exciting world of cooking. The following chapter contains recipes that employ many of the techniques discussed in the preceding pages. As you test your culinary prowess, think about everything we've talked about so far: about the sensory experience, about the advantages of cooking, about shopping smart for groceries, about cooking in layers and experimenting with new recipes. And if I may say, pretty soon, you'll find cooking to be as limitless, flexible and enjoyable as I do. And hopefully, you'll give your own kitchen a serious consideration before heading out for those daily bites.

Welcome to the newest restaurant in your neighborhood.

Welcome home.

Chapter 4 Takeaways

The 3 stages of cooking:
- Prepping ingredients (identify the ingredients you need, chop ingredients in advance if necessary & marinate meats to add flavor)
- Cooking in layers (build the flavor foundation, add ingredients in descending order of cooking time & allow time to bring the dish together)
- Assembling the dish

Watch out for:
- Always cooking on high heat (is it really necessary?)
- Using excessive amounts of spices (you want to taste the main ingredient, not just the spices)
- Maintaining cleanliness in the kitchen – it is sacrosanct!

Part II
The Workshop

5
Recipes

THE RECIPES THAT FOLLOW represent a collection
of ideas that I have used over the years to create new meals
everyday. Among the wide variety represented here, you'll find
recipes on appetizers, main courses, breakfast dishes, desserts and
even suggestions on how to use leftovers. Be assured that most of
these recipes have taken the form of finger foods at keg parties,
entrées at dinner soirees, energizing breakfasts on weekends, quick-
fixes for the late night munchies, etc. Some have been featured in
the cookbooks offered by Seattle's public television channel as part
of their fundraising efforts.

Additionally, each recipe follows the ideas presented in this book – about cooking healthy, saving money, cooking in layers, experimenting with new ingredients, different cooking styles, etc. Each recipe is presented in a readable fashion in a template form with ingredient lists, cookware suggestion, and clear instructions on how to go through the different stages of prepping, cooking and serving the dish. Each recipe also indicates how long it takes to prep and cook the dish and the level of difficulty from easy to difficult. A sample template is presented on the next page for clarification.

I found that the best way to organize recipes was by meal course, and within each section, by vegetarian or meat dishes. Here are the major sections:

1. Breakfast
2. Vegetarian dishes
3. Meat dishes
4. Wraps
5. Soups and stews
6. Rice, noodles & pasta dishes

Many of these recipes can be altered slightly to make fabulous finger food platters for parties. The table on the next page provides a handy summary of ingredients, flavors and cooking styles for various cuisines. This table provides a powerful way for changing some recipes from one cuisine to another.

With that, let's dive right in and turn up the heat!

Cooking Tips by Cuisine/Dish

This table is a powerful guide for changing some recipes in this section (particularly meat dishes) – e.g., to change a recipe from "Indian" to "Italian", simply change each component presented in the rows below from one cuisine to the other.

	INDIAN	CHINESE	THAI	ITALIAN	SOUP
Flavor base	Onion, peppers, garlic, ginger	Onion, peppers, garlic, ginger	Onion, peppers, garlic, ginger	Onion, peppers, garlic	Onion, celery, peppers, carrots, garlic, ginger
Spices	Garam masala, curry powder, cumin, turmeric, chili powder	Chili powder, sesame seeds, Asian seasoning, chili flakes	Thai curry paste, chili flakes	Mustard, black pepper, Italian seasoning, chili flakes	Black pepper, chili flakes, curry powder
Herbs	Cilantro, curry leaves, bay leaves	Cilantro, basil	Basil, kaffir lime leaves	Parsley, basil	Bay leaves, cilantro, parsley
Sauce	Tomato sauce	Soy sauce, sesame oil	Coconut milk	Tomato sauce, cream, balsamic vinegar	Stock, broth, water
Chop style	Diced	Julienne	Rough	Diced, Rough	Diced, Chunky
Flame	Medium	High	Medium to High	Medium	Low to Medium
Garnish	Cilantro	Cilantro	Nuts	Parsley	Herbs
Side/Base	Basmati Rice or Nan	Rice or Asian noodles	Jasmine Rice	Pasta	Crackers or croutons

RECIPE TEMPLATE

The recipes that follow are presented according to the following template, which provides the name of the recipe, the time required and the level of difficulty of the dish. You'll then see a list of ingredients, the suggested cookware and detailed instructions on how to prepare the dish.

recipe title

Time = prep time + cook time (difficulty)

Ingredients
List of ingredients

Optional
List of optional ingredients

Cookware
Recommended type of cookware

Prep
This is stage #1 of cooking: Most common tasks presented here are chopping ingredients and marinating (for meats)

Method
This is stage #2 of cooking: This section will tell you how to build a flavor base, add ingredients in layers and finally bring the dish together.

Serving
This is stage #3 of cooking: This section will tell you how to present the dish, suggest side dishes and beverages to complement.

NOTE:
- Prep & Cook times are mentioned in m = minutes and h = hours
- Difficulty is mentioned as E = Easy, M = Medium, D = Difficult
- Example: **Time = 5m + 10m (M)** refers to a dish that takes 5 minutes of prep time, 10 minutes of cook time and is of medium difficulty
- Also note that the above template is the format in which most recipes are written, but not all sections presented above are always mentioned in the recipes that follow.

BREAKFAST

Breakfast is unquestionably the most important meal of the day. Most of the recipes presented here are quick to prepare and easy on the difficulty scale (crepes will take a little practice, but you will soon be flipping them like a pro!). Enjoy these recipes on weekend mornings for breakfast or on Sundays for brunch, or, if you love breakfast dishes as much as I do, on any day and any time! The last three recipes are also excellent as desserts at the end of a meal.

Recipe	Time	Difficulty
• Scrambled eggs	5m + 10m	Easy
• Spinach & mushroom omelet	5m + 10m	Easy
• French toast	5m + 15m	Easy
• Crepes	1h + 10m	Medium
• Crepes w/ chocolate spread	10m	Medium
• Fruit salad	10m	Easy

scrambled eggs

Ingredients
3-4 eggs (or equivalent egg substitute)
½ tbsp butter or extra light olive oil
¼ red onion, diced
1 Serrano, diced
¼ green bell pepper, diced
¼ red bell pepper, diced
¼ roma tomato, diced
Salt and pepper, to taste
Tabasco sauce for a kick
Chopped cilantro

Optional
2 shitake mushrooms, thinly sliced
¼ zucchini, diced

Cookware
11" Wok

Prep
Chop the onions, peppers, tomato, mushrooms, zucchini and cilantro. Beat the eggs with a whisk until fluffy (add a splash of milk and a touch of flour if necessary).

Method
Heat the butter or oil in a skillet. Add the onions and peppers. Sprinkle a little salt and pepper. Toss the ingredients to mix well and cook for about a minute. Next, add the mushrooms and zucchini and cook for two more minutes. Then add the diced tomato and cook for 30 seconds. Now add the beaten eggs and rapidly mix it with the other ingredients to break the eggs. Continue this motion until the eggs have set. Mix in the chopped cilantro.

Serving
Serve with toasted bread, low-fat butter and coffee.

spinach & mushroom omelet

Ingredients

3-4 eggs (or equivalent amount of egg substitute)
A handful of spinach, thoroughly washed & finely chopped
4 assorted mushrooms (shitake, oyster, crimini, chanterelle all work great)
1 tbsp butter or extra light olive oil
¼ red onion, diced
1 Serrano, diced
Salt and pepper, to taste
Tabasco sauce for a kick
Chopped cilantro

Optional

¼ green bell pepper, diced
¼ red bell pepper, diced
¼ roma tomato, diced
¼ zucchini, diced
Grated cheese to taste

Cookware

12" Omelet pan, nonstick

Prep

Chop the onions, peppers, tomato, mushrooms, zucchini, spinach and cilantro. Beat the eggs with a whisk until fluffy (add a splash of milk and a touch of flour if necessary).

Method

Heat the butter or oil in a skillet. Add the onions and peppers. Sprinkle a little salt and pepper. Toss the ingredients to mix well and cook for a minute. Next, add the spinach, mushrooms and zucchini and cook for two more minutes. When the mushrooms and spinach have cooked through (spinach should turn a beautiful bright green, and the mushrooms should become a little shiny), distribute the contents evenly throughout the omelet pan. Now gently pour the beaten eggs and shake the pan to distribute it evenly throughout the pan. Sprinkle with some salt and pepper if necessary, and let the eggs set. Sprinkle with the chopped cilantro when the eggs are almost done, and turn the heat off. Sprinkle some cheese and fold the omelet over in half. Let rest for 30 seconds and remove omelet from the skillet onto a plate.

Serving
Serve with toasted bread, low-fat butter and coffee.

french toast

Time = 5m + 15m (E)

Ingredients
    3-4 eggs (or equivalent amount of egg substitute)
    4 slices of a fresh loaf of white bread
    ¼ cup fat-free milk
    1 tbsp sugar (granulated or powered)
    1 tbsp butter or extra light olive oil
    Salt, to taste

Optional
    A splash of amaretto

Cookware
    12" Omelet pan, nonstick

Prep
Beat the eggs, milk, amaretto and sugar with a whisk until fluffy. Cut off edges from bread slices.

Method
Heat the butter or oil in a skillet. When the oil is reasonably hot (not smoking), dip the bread slices in the egg bath one at a time, and add to the hot pan. It is a good idea to do only two slices at a time to not crowd the pan. Let the bread cook for 30-60 seconds on each side or until golden brown. Remove onto a plate.

Serving

There are several ways to serve French toast. The simplest way is to layer them on the plate as a stack of pancakes and dust with powdered sugar (or serve with your favorite syrup). Alternatively, stack the pieces and cut them along the diagonal, and stack each row to serve family style. Serve with a pot of hot coffee.

crepes (sweet and savory)

Time = 1h + 10m (M)

Ingredients for Sweet Crepes
   1 cup flour
   1 cup skim milk
   1 egg (or egg substitute)
   A splash of vanilla
   2-3 tbsp Amaretto liqueur (or substitute with your favorite liqueur)
   1-2 tsp powered sugar

Ingredients for Savory Crepes
   1 cup flour
   1 cup skim milk
   1 egg (or egg substitute)
   A sprinkling of chopped Cilantro leaves (or other favorite herb)
   1 tsp cumin seeds
   A splash of Tabasco
   Salt & Pepper to taste

Cookware
   10" crepe pan (OR skillet), nonstick

Prep

Combine all the ingredients in a bowl to make the crepe batter. If you have a mixer (or even a whisk), use it to remove any lumps in the batter. Cover and refrigerate the batter for at least an hour.

Method

Place the crepe pan on high heat. Coat the pan with some butter. The pan should be hot enough to cause the butter to bubble. Ladle the batter onto the pan and swirl it around to cover the entire area of the pan. You may have to add more batter to do this, but only add enough batter to make a thin crepe. After the batter has settled and no longer moving, wait for at least 30 seconds. When the edges of the crepe are nicely formed and begin to loosen, it's time to flip. Use a flat spatula to loosen the edges and body of the crepe, and flip! If you are not comfortable flipping the crepe with a quick wrist motion, use the spatula. Once flipped, allow the crepe to cook for 30 seconds on the other side. Remove from the pan onto a plate and continue making more crepes.

crepes w/ chocolate hazelnut spread

Time = 10m (M)

For the filling & garnish
  1 banana, sliced into rounds throughout its length
     -OR- use a handful of slivered almonds for the filling
  Your favorite chocolate hazelnut spread
  Powered Sugar for garnish

Prep

Peel and slice the banana into thin rounds lengthwise.

Method

Make sweet crepes as described before. Coat one side of the crepe with a desired amount of chocolate-hazelnut spread. Then add banana slices along the diameter of the crepe and fold it like a burrito. If using almonds, then sprinkle with slivered almonds over the spread. Do the same thing with a second crepe, except add the banana slices or slivered almonds on one quarter of the crepe and fold it like a triangle.

Serving

Arrange the crepes on your serving plate and given them a light sprinkling of powdered sugar. Enjoy with a freshly brewed cup of hot coffee or a tall glass of fresh-extracted fruit juice.

fruit salad

Ingredients
1 apple, cored & thinly sliced
1 orange, peeled & thinly sliced
1 banana, thinly sliced
2 tbsp honey
A handful of chopped walnuts

Optional
1 pear, cored & thinly sliced
1 kiwi, peeled & thinly sliced
4 large strawberries, thinly sliced
1 more banana, thinly sliced

Cookware
Salad bowl (to combine ingredients)

Prep
Chop all the fruits one by one as instructed. Next, chop the walnuts into small pieces).

Method
Combine all the chopped fruits in a salad bowl. Add the honey and mix to coat all the fruits evenly. Now add the chopped walnuts and mix through.

Serving
Serve individual portions in small bowls. This salad is best eaten after a meal.

VEGETARIAN DISHES

With vegetarianism growing in popularity every year, I decided to include a number of recipes here that draw from Indian and Asian influences. The recipes presented here are along assorted levels of difficulty, but easy to master with practice.

Recipe	Time	Difficulty
• Paneer	Overnight	Difficult
• Paneer & peas curry	10m + 15m	Medium
• Potato spinach curry	10m + 25m	Medium
• Potato cauliflower curry	10m + 25m	Medium
• Spicy okra	10m + 15m	Medium
• Garbanzo beans w/ spinach	10m + 20m	Easy
• Red beans w/ mushrooms	10m + 15m	Easy
• Vegetable stir-fry	10m + 10m	Easy
• Green beans w/ walnuts	10m + 10m	Easy

paneer (indian cottage cheese)

Ingredients
 ½ gallon milk (2% or higher fat content)
 1 tbsp limejuice
 2 tbsp vinegar

Cookware
 5 qt saucepan, nonstick

Method
Heat the milk in a saucepan until it is close to boiling. Add the limejuice
& vinegar. The milk should now start to curdle. Stir the milk gently,
adding more limejuice and vinegar if it hasn't started to curdle. Let it rest
for a few minutes to separate the whey from the curd. Remove the curd
into some cheesecloth, rest the cheesecloth in a container and put some
weight directly above it. Refrigerate for up to 5 hours. Paneer is now
ready to be used in recipes.

Alternatively, Paneer is also available in Indian grocery stores.

paneer & peas curry (mutter paneer)

Time – 10m + 15m (M)

Ingredients
 1 tbsp extra virgin olive oil
 ½ red onion, chopped
 1 Serrano, chopped
 ½ green bell pepper, chopped
 ½ red bell pepper, chopped
 1 large clove of garlic, finely chopped
 ½ inch piece of ginger, finely chopped
 Frozen Peas - 2 handfuls
 Paneer cut in cubes (or strips)
 1 tsp garam masala
 Salt, to taste
 ½ tsp of balsamic vinegar

4 tbsp of milk (or cream or butter)
Chopped cilantro

Cookware
12" sauté pan, nonstick

Prep
Chop the onions, peppers, garlic and ginger. Next, chop the paneer into bite size pieces.

Method
Heat the olive oil in a saucepan. Add the onions, peppers, garlic, ginger and a little salt. Toss the ingredients to mix well and cook for a minute. Add the garam masala and toss to mix again. Add the paneer cubes & peas and toss again. Cook this for 5 to 7 minutes. Add the milk (or cream or butter) and mix well. Add the balsamic vinegar. Sprinkle with chopped cilantro and toss the ingredients.

Serving
This dish is eaten best with Naan or Chappatis (both Indian breads). Basmati rice or pilaf is a good side to this dish as well.

potato spinach curry (alu palak)

Time = 10m + 25m (M)

Ingredients
1 tbsp extra virgin olive oil, for the sauté pan
½ onion, thinly sliced
2 cloves of fresh garlic, finely chopped
½ inch piece of fresh ginger, finely chopped
½ red bell pepper, diced
2 Serrano peppers, diced
2 white Yukon potatoes quartered lengthwise and thinly sliced
1 head of spinach, washed & chopped
3 roma tomatoes cut lengthwise in strips
1 tsp garam masala
Salt to taste
Chopped cilantro leaves

Cookware
12" sauté pan, nonstick

Prep
Chop the onions, peppers, garlic and ginger. Next, peel the potatoes and chop into bite size pieces. Next, thoroughly wash and chop the spinach.

Method
Heat the olive oil in a sauté pan. Add the onions, garlic & ginger. Add a pinch of salt to help the cooking. After 15 seconds or so, add the garam masala, the Serrano chilies and red bell pepper. Toss the ingredients around the pan and cook for about a minute. When the onions & peppers get a shiny color, add the potato slices and toss them around the pan. Add more salt if necessary. If the pan dries out, add a little water. Add the spinach and toss it to mix well with the other ingredients. The spinach should give out more water and cook down. When the pan dries out, add the tomatoes and the cilantro leaves mix well and continue cooking. Add ½ cup of water toward the end and cook on low heat until the potatoes are completely cooked. Let rest for a few minutes.

Serving
This potato-spinach curry goes well with steamed Basmati rice or hot Naans and a side of plain fat-free yogurt.

potato cauliflower curry (alu gobi)

Time = 10m + 25m (M)

Ingredients
  1 tbsp extra virgin olive oil, for the sauté pan
  1 tsp cumin seeds
  ½ onion, thinly sliced
  2 cloves of fresh garlic, finely chopped
  ½ inch piece of fresh ginger, finely chopped
  ½ red bell pepper, diced
  2 Serrano peppers, diced
  2 white Yukon potatoes roughly chopped
  1 head of spinach, washed & chopped

2 tbsp tomato paste
1 tsp chili powder
1 tsp turmeric powder
1 tsp crushed red pepper flakes
Salt to taste
Chopped cilantro leaves

Cookware
12" sauté pan, nonstick

Prep
Chop the onions, peppers, garlic and ginger. Next, peel and chop the potatoes into bite size pieces. Next, chop the cauliflower into bite size pieces. To cut the cauliflower, it is best to cut the flower into two pieces and then start cutting at the bottom of the flowerets. Doing so will eventually separate the whole flower into individual flowerets.

Method
Heat the olive oil in a sauté pan. Add the cumin, onions, garlic & ginger. Add a pinch of salt to help the cooking. After 15 seconds or so, add the garam masala, the Serrano chilies and red bell pepper. Toss the ingredients around the pan and cook for about a minute. When the onions & peppers get a shiny color, add the tomato paste, chili powder, turmeric and crushed red pepper flakes. Mix well. After a few seconds, add water and turn the heat to medium and let the flavor base build. After about 2 minutes, add the potato slices and coat thoroughly with the tomato flavor base. Add more salt if necessary. If the pan dries out, add a little water. When the potatoes have cooked for about 15 minutes, add the cauliflower flowerets and mix well. If the pan dries out, add just enough water so nothing sticks to the bottom of the pan. Cook on medium heat until the potatoes and cauliflower are completely cooked. Let rest for a few minutes and sprinkle with the chopped cilantro.

Serving
Alu gobi goes well with steamed Basmati rice or hot Naans and a side of plain fat-free yogurt.

spicy okra (bhindi masala)

Ingredients

2 tbsp extra virgin olive oil, for the sauté pan
1 pound okra, trimmed and chopped in halves
½ onion, thinly sliced
2 cloves of fresh garlic, finely chopped
½ inch piece of fresh ginger, finely chopped
½ red bell pepper, diced
2 Serrano peppers, diced
3 roma tomatoes cut lengthwise
2 tsp garam masala
1 tsp chili powder
1 tsp turmeric powder
1 tsp tamarind paste
Salt to taste
Chopped cilantro leaves

Cookware

12" sauté pan, nonstick

Prep

Chop the onions, peppers, garlic and ginger. Next, trim the edges of the okra and cut In halves by slicing at an angle.

Method

Heat the olive oil in the sauté pan. Add the onions, garlic & ginger. Add a pinch of salt to help the cooking. When the onions become shiny, add the garam masala, the Serrano chilies and red bell pepper. Cook for about a minute. Add the okra pieces and the chili powder and turmeric. Toss the okra pieces to coat with all the spices evenly. Cook on medium heat until the pan dries out and the okra becomes slightly blackened. At this stage, add the tomatoes, the tamarind paste and the cilantro leaves; mix well and continue cooking. If you want a little gravy, add water and continue to cook on low heat. Otherwise, for a more traditional okra masala, turn the heat to low and cook until the okras are cooked all the way through. Let rest for a few minutes.

Serving
This okra masala goes with Naans or Chappatis, or as a side for vegetable pilaf.

garbanzo beans w/ spinach (chole palak)

Time = 10m + 20m (E)

Ingredients
1 tbsp extra virgin olive oil, for the sauté pan
½ onion, thinly sliced
2 cloves of fresh garlic, finely chopped
½ inch piece of fresh ginger, finely chopped
½ red bell pepper, julienne
½ habanero pepper, julienne
2 cans Garbanzo beans, washed and dried
1 head of spinach, washed & chopped
1 roma tomato, cut lengthwise in strips
1 tsp turmeric powder
1 tsp chili powder
Salt to taste
Chopped cilantro leaves

Optional
1 tbsp grated coconut

Cookware
12" sauté pan, nonstick

Prep
Chop the onions, peppers, garlic and ginger. Chop the roma tomato.

Method
Heat the olive oil in a sauté pan. Add the onions, garlic & ginger. Add a pinch of salt to help the cooking. After 15 seconds or so, add the chili powder, turmeric and red bell pepper. Toss the ingredients around the pan and cook for about a minute. When the onions & peppers get a shiny color, add the garbanzo beans. Add more salt if necessary. If the pan dries out, add a little water. Add the spinach and toss it to mix well with the other ingredients. The spinach will "sweat" (give out water) and

cook down. When the pan has almost dried out, add the tomatoes and the cilantro leaves mix well and continue cooking. Add ½ cup of water toward the end and cook on low heat until all the ingredients are completely cooked. Sprinkle grated coconut and mix well. Let rest for a few minutes.

Serving
This garbanzo beans curry goes well with Naan or steamed Basmati rice and a side of plain fat-free yogurt.

red kidney beans w/ mushrooms

Time = 10m + 10m (E)

Ingredients
1tbsp extra virgin olive oil, for the sauté pan
½ onion, thinly sliced
2 cloves of fresh garlic, finely chopped
½ inch piece of fresh ginger, finely chopped
½ habanero pepper, julienne
2 cans dark red kidney beans, washed and dried
6 shitake mushrooms, thinly sliced
2 tbsp tomato paste
1 tsp turmeric powder
1 tsp chili powder
1 tsp garam masala
Salt to taste
Chopped cilantro leaves

Cookware
12" sauté pan, nonstick

Prep
Chop the onions, peppers, garlic and ginger. Chop the shitake mushrooms by slicing each mushroom to create strips.

Method

Heat the olive oil in a sauté pan. Add the cumin, onions, garlic & ginger. Add a pinch of salt to help the cooking. After 15 seconds or so, add the garam masala, the Serrano chilies and red bell pepper. Toss the ingredients around the pan and cook for about a minute. When the onions & peppers get a shiny color, add the tomato paste, chili powder, turmeric and crushed red pepper flakes. Mix well. After a few seconds, add water and turn the heat to medium and let the flavor base build. Add the beans, coat and let cook for about 10 minutes. Next, add the mushrooms, mix thoroughly and cook for another 10 minutes. Sprinkle with chopped cilantro to finish the dish.

Serving

This red beans and mushroom curry goes well with Naan or steamed Basmati rice and a side of plain fat-free yogurt.

vegetable stir-fry

Time = 10m + 10m (E)

Ingredients

1 tbsp extra virgin olive oil
1 tsp sesame oil
½ red onion, julienne
1 large clove of garlic, finely chopped
½ inch piece of ginger, finely chopped
¼ habanero pepper, finely chopped
¼ green bell pepper, julienne
¼ red bell pepper, julienne
¼ yellow bell pepper, julienne
3 shitake (or button) mushrooms, thinly sliced
10 broccoli flowerets
¼ head small green cabbage, thinly chopped
2 tbsp low-sodium soy sauce
1 tsp hoi sin sauce
Salt and pepper, to taste
Chopped cilantro
Bok Choy, thinly chopped

Prep
Chop the onions, celery, peppers, garlic and ginger. Chop all vegetables in thin strips (julienne) or at an angle to add character to the dish. If making a meat stir-fry, cut the meat into thin strips. Sprinkle your favorite spices (salt, pepper, chili powder, etc) to coat the meat strips. Then, dredge the meat pieces in some flour for a crispy texture when cooked.

Method
The key to a great stir-fry is to have all the ingredients pre-cut and ready to roll. The rest is quick and easy. Place a wok on high-heat. When it is just under smoking, add the olive oil. Now add the ingredients one by one, stirring rapidly. Allow less than 10 seconds for any ingredient to sit untouched in the wok. Add the onions, garlic & ginger. Add a pinch of salt and pepper. Stir. Add the peppers – green, red, yellow & habanero. Now add the broccoli. Wait until the broccoli start to turn a brighter shade of green, and then add the cabbage and mushrooms. Toss the ingredients in the wok and then add the bok choy. Deglaze with the soy sauce and hoi sin. Add the sesame oil. Stir the contents rapidly once again and sprinkle with cilantro leaves. Toss & serve immediately!

With meat
If you're adding meat to the stir-fry, make sure your meat Is cut in thin short strips. Add the meat *before* you add any vegetables. This is important because meat takes longer to cook than vegetables.

Serving
Stir-fry goes great with yakisoba noodles or just steamed rice.

green beans w/ walnuts

Time = 10m + 10m (E)

Ingredients
3 tbsp extra virgin olive oil
1 lb green beans, edges trimmed and halved at an angle
Handful of Walnuts

¼ red onion, diced
4 large cloves of garlic, finely chopped
½ inch piece of ginger, finely chopped
Crushed red pepper flakes, to taste
Salt and pepper, to taste
1 tsp honey
Chopped basil

Cookware
11" Wok

Prep
Chop the onions, garlic and ginger. Trim the edges from the green beans and slice into halves at an angle. Chop the walnuts into bite-size pieces. Chop the basil leaves.

Method
Place a wok on high-heat. When it is just under smoking, add the olive oil. Now add the onion, garlic and ginger. Sauté for a few seconds, then add the green beans, salt, pepper and red chili flakes. Toss the ingredients for a few minutes, until the beans take on a deep green color. Now add the walnuts, toss well together with the beans, then add the honey and toss again to mix thoroughly. Sprinkle with the chopped basil.

Serving
This dish is perfect as a side/appetizer. Serve in a small bowl as an accompaniment to a main dish.

MEAT DISHES

Here are a number of recipes with different kinds of meat: beef, pork, chicken and fish. As mentioned in Part I of this book, each recipe has different requirements for marinating, cooking and serving. As you cook these dishes repeatedly, you'll soon develop your own recipes. Turn to these recipes for preparing hearty meals.

Recipe	Time	Difficulty
Chicken curry	15m + 25m	Medium
Chicken w/ cabbage & mushrooms	15m + 15m	Medium
Chicken w/ chinese string beans	15m + 20m	Medium
Ground lamb or beef w/ peas	10m + 35m	Medium
Crepes w/ kheema and yogurt	Various	Medium
Spice-rubbed crusty pork tenderloin	15m + 40m	Difficult
Chicken kofta	15m + 40m	Difficult
Tandoori chicken	Overnight	Medium
Spicy chicken finger food	15m + 20m	Medium
Salmon filet	3m + 10m	Easy
Salmon dill toast	5m + 15m	Easy
Pork and broccoli	15m + 20m	Easy

chicken curry

Ingredients

3 boneless skinless chicken thighs, cut in chunks
4 chicken drumsticks, skinned and trimmed of excess fat
2 tbsp extra virgin olive oil
½ red onion, julienne
3 large cloves of garlic, finely chopped
1 inch piece of ginger, finely chopped
¼ habanero pepper, finely chopped
¼ green bell pepper, julienne
½ lime, fresh squeezed
1 tsp meat masala
1 tsp chili powder
1 tsp turmeric powder
1 tsp garam masala
1 small cinnamon stick
1 tsp cumin seeds
¼ 6 oz can tomato paste
¼ 12 oz can diced tomatoes
Salt and pepper, to taste
Chopped cilantro

Cookware

12" sauté pan, nonstick

Prep

Start by skinning the chicken pieces and trimming off fat and "silver skin". Cut the chicken thighs into large chunks, but leave the drumsticks whole. Start the marinade with most of the chopped garlic and ginger. Then add the meat masala, garam masala, chili powder, turmeric powder, salt, fresh squeezed lime juice and half the cumin seeds. Add a tbsp of olive oil and some cilantro leaves. Mix well to create a spicy mixture. Now add the chicken and coat completely. Set aside in the refrigerator for 3-5 hours.

Method

Heat ½ tbsp olive oil in the sauté pan. Add the marinated chicken and fry until all the pieces are evenly browned, about 2 minutes. Remove the chicken from the pan into a bowl. To the same pan, add the remaining ½ tbsp of olive oil. Add the remaining ginger and garlic, the onions, all peppers, and the rest of the cumin seeds. Add a pinch of salt and fry until the contents of the pan gain a persistent shine. Now add the tomato paste, diced tomatoes and some water. Mix thoroughly, cover and cook on medium heat until the flavor base comes together. Now add the chicken back to the pan and cook on medium heat for about 20 minutes, stirring occasionally so the contents don't stick to the bottom of the pan. Add a little water if the pan is too dry. Cook until the chicken is completely done (should not be pink on the inside). Sprinkle with cilantro leaves and serve immediately.

Serving

Ladle chicken curry over steamed basmati rice or serve with hot Naans or Chappatis.

chicken w/ cabbage & mushrooms

Time = 15m + 15m (M)

Ingredients

2 chicken breasts, skinned, boned & chopped in strips
½ head of crisp green cabbage, washed & shredded
8 mushrooms (assorted), roughly chopped
1 tbsp extra virgin olive oil, for the sauté pan
1 tsp sesame oil, for flavor
1 tsp soy sauce
½ lime, juiced by squeezing
½ onion, thinly sliced
2 cloves of fresh garlic, finely chopped
½ inch piece of fresh ginger, finely chopped
½ red bell pepper, diced
2 Serrano peppers, diced
Salt and pepper to taste
Chopped cilantro leaves

Prep
In a bowl, mix together sesame oil, limejuice, some cilantro leaves, salt and pepper. Add the chicken pieces and coat very well. Set aside for at least 15 minutes.

Method
Heat the olive oil in a sauté pan. Add the onions, garlic & ginger. Add a pinch of salt to help the cooking. After 15 seconds or so, add the Serrano chilies and red bell pepper. Toss the ingredients around the pan and cook for about a minute. When the onions & peppers get a shiny color, add chicken pieces. Season with salt and pepper. If the pan dries out, add a little water. Cook until the chicken is almost done. Now add the mushrooms and shredded cabbage. Mix well with the other ingredients. At this point, add the soy sauce and cook for a few minutes, until the cabbage wilts down a little and a gains a coating of all the oils & flavors from the pot. Sprinkle with cilantro leaves, and let rest for a few minutes.

Serving
This dish goes with steamed Jasmine rice. It also goes really well inside a savory crepe, or with Chappatis or Naans.

chicken w/ chinese string beans

Time = 15m + 15m (M)

Ingredients
½ lb ground chicken
1 lb Chinese string beans
2 tbsp extra virgin olive oil, for the sauté pan
1 tsp sesame oil, for flavor
1 tbsp soy sauce

½ lime, juiced by squeezing
½ onion, thinly sliced
2 cloves of fresh garlic, finely chopped
½ inch piece of fresh ginger, finely chopped
½ red bell pepper, diced
2 Serrano peppers, diced
Salt and pepper to taste
Chopped cilantro leaves

Optional
Substitute sesame oil with 1 tsp your favorite curry powder

Cookware
12" sauté pan, nonstick
OR Wok, nonstick

Prep
Trim the string beans on the edges and slice at an angle, cutting into 5-6 pieces along the length. Wash the beans thoroughly. Cut the onions, garlic, ginger, peppers and cilantro leaves.

Method
Heat the olive oil in a sauté pan. Add the onions, garlic & ginger. Add a pinch of salt to help the cooking. After 15 seconds or so, add the Serrano chilies and red bell pepper. Toss them around the pan and cook for about a minute. When the onions & peppers get a shiny color, add the ground chicken. Break up the chicken and mix thoroughly. Season with salt, pepper, chili flakes and your favorite spices. If the pan dries out, add a splash of soy sauce and water. Cook until the chicken is almost done. Now add the string beans. Mix well with the other ingredients. Cook for just a few minutes, until the chicken is completely cooked and the string beans develop a deep green color. Sprinkle with cilantro leaves and let rest for a few minutes.

Serving
This dish goes with steamed Jasmine rice.

ground lamb or beef w/ peas (kheema)

Ingredients
2 lbs leanest ground lamb or beef
¼ cup frozen green peas
2 tbsp extra virgin olive oil
¼ red onion, diced
¼ green pepper, diced
3 cloves of garlic, finely chopped
½ inch piece of ginger, finely chopped
2 tbsp tomato paste
1 roma tomato, diced
1 tsp cumin seeds
1 tsp chili powder
1 tsp turmeric powder
1 tsp garam masala
1 tsp meat masala
1 tbsp red pepper flakes
Salt & pepper to taste
Chopped cilantro

Cookware
5 qt sauce pan

Prep
Chop the onions, green peppers, garlic, ginger, tomato and cilantro.

Method
Heat the olive oil in a sauce pan. Add the ground lamb or beef and sauté until the meat has browned. Remove the beef into a bowl and add onions, cumin seeds, garlic, ginger and peppers to the same sauce pan. Add a pinch of salt to help the cooking. After about a minute, add the garam masala, meat masala, chili powder, turmeric, red chili flakes and the tomato paste and cook on medium heat for a few minutes. If the pan dries out, add a little water to help it along if necessary. When the sauce has come to a good consistency, add the beef back to the sauce pan, and add any remaining seasoning. Cook until the beef is almost done. Now add the green peas, sprinkle with more salt and pepper and mix

76

well and cook for 15 minutes or until the beef is completely cooked. Sprinkle with cilantro leaves, and let rest for a few minutes.

Serving
This dish goes with steamed Basmati rice and a side of plain fat-free yogurt. It also goes really well inside a savory crepe, or with Chappatis or Naans.

crepes w/ kheema and yogurt

Time = Various (M)

For the filling & garnish
  Kheema – desired amount
  Chopped cilantro leaves
  Freshly cracked black pepper

Method
Make savory crepes and kheema separately. Fill two crepes with kheema and fold like burritos. Top the crepes with a dollop of plain yogurt, or spread the yogurt thinly over the crepes.

Serving
Arrange the crepes on your serving plate and given them a light sprinkling of freshly cracked black pepper and chopped cilantro leaves. Enjoy with your favorite merlot.

spice-rubbed crusty pork tenderloin

Time = 15m + 40m (D)

Ingredients
  1 pork tenderloin, trimmed of excess fat
  ½ bunch of spinach, de-stemmed and thoroughly washed
  ¼ cup all-purpose flour
  3 tbsp extra virgin olive oil
  ½ red onion, julienne
  3 large cloves of garlic, finely chopped
  1 inch piece of ginger, finely chopped
  ¼ habanero pepper, finely chopped

½ lime, fresh squeezed
1 tsp meat masala
1 tsp chili powder
1 tsp turmeric powder
1 tsp garam masala
Salt and pepper, to taste
Chopped cilantro
Cilantro sprigs (or chives, if you prefer) for garnish

Cookware
12" sauté pan (ovenproof to 400 ºF), nonstick

Prep
Start by trimming the tenderloin of fat and "silver skin". Score the meat at various points across the width of the tenderloin and set aside. Start the marinade with most of the chopped garlic and ginger. Then add the meat masala, garam masala, chili powder, turmeric powder, salt, fresh squeezed limejuice. Add 1 tbsp of olive oil and some cilantro leaves. Mix well to create a spicy mixture. Now add the tenderloin and coat completely, making sure the marinate gets into all those crevices. Set aside in the refrigerator 8-10 hours.

Method
Begin by preheating the oven to 400 ºF. Pour the flour onto a big plate. Mix in 1 tsp of meat masala and 1 tsp of chili powder and set aside. Remove the tenderloin from the refrigerator and thaw (covered) at room temperature for a few minutes. Dredge the tenderloin in the seasoned flour, coating on all sides, and shake off any excess flour. Heat 1tbsp olive oil in the sauté pan. Add the tenderloin and sear on medium-high heat until all sides are evenly browned. Use the remaining olive oil as necessary to assist the browning. When the tenderloin has been browned evenly on all sides, transfer the sauté pan to the oven. Let the pork cook in the oven for 25-30 minutes or until the meat is no longer pink on the inside (to test this, cut the meat a third of way in the center, being careful not to cut too much to release the juices). Remove from the oven and set aside for 5-10 minutes. Carve the meat into about 10 pieces across the length of the tenderloin. In the same pan, add some olive oil and sauté the spinach, adding just a pinch of salt and pepper.

This will make the foundation on which to lay the pieces of tenderloin. To make a pan sauce, deglaze the pan with ½ cup of red wine and reduce it by half. Optionally, add a ½ tbsp of butter and stir it through, cooking for another 10 seconds. If you're adventurous, you could use the remaining flour from coating the tenderloin to make a roux with some butter before adding the wine. This makes a basic pan sauce.

Serving

If serving family style, arrange the tenderloin on a big serving platter. Drizzle the pan sauce on top. Garnish with sprigs of cilantro leaves on either side to create a family style serving. If serving Individual portions, create a bed of sautéed spinach on each plate. Add two pieces of tenderloin and drizzle the pan sauce on top. Garnish with two crossing sprigs of cilantro leaves or chives.

chicken kofta

Time = 15m + 40m (D)

Ingredients
2 lbs ground chicken
1 egg (or egg substitute)
¼ cup breadcrumbs
¼ cup all-purpose flour
2 tbsp extra virgin olive oil
¼ red onion, diced
¼ green pepper, diced (or cut in chunks)
¼ red pepper, diced (or cut in chunks)
3 large cloves of garlic, finely chopped
1 inch piece of ginger, finely chopped
1 green chili, finely chopped
2 roma tomatoes, diced
½ lime, fresh squeezed
2 tsp meat masala (if available)
2 tsp chili powder
2 tsp garam masala
Salt and pepper, to taste
Chopped cilantro leaves

Optional
  1 can (6 oz or smaller), tomato paste
  1 can (6 oz or smaller), tomato puree

Cookware
  12" nonstick sauté pan
  Casserole dish

Prep

In a salad bowl, combine the chicken with the eggs, the garlic, ginger, garam masala, chili powder, meat masala (or your favorite spices), cilantro, chilies, limejuice, salt and pepper. Add ½ tbsp of olive oil, and mix well. Now add the breadcrumbs until the mixture reaches a firm consistency that will hold shape when rolled into balls. Roll the mixture into balls (like meatballs) and set aside. Pour the all-purpose flour into another bowl, and season with some garam masala. Carefully dredge each chicken ball in the flour, and re-press the balls, making sure they aren't sticky to the touch. Allow the chicken balls to set by putting them in the refrigerator for an hour.

Method

Begin by preheating the oven to 250°F-300°F. Heat some oil in the sauté pan. Remove the chicken balls from the fridge. When the oil is hot, add the chicken pieces to the pan in batches. When the balls have been browned on all sides, remove into the casserole dish. Transfer the casserole dish to the oven, and bake for 25-30 minutes (or until the chicken is cooked all the way through). Meanwhile, in the sauté pan, add a little more oil, and add the rest of the garlic & ginger. Make sure you scrape all the bits of flour and chicken left from browning the chicken in the pan. These bits will thicken the sauce. Now add the onions and the peppers and season with salt, pepper and the remaining spices. Cook for 2-3 minutes. Now add the tomatoes (and the tomato puree or tomato paste if that suits your taste), and simmer until all the ingredients are cooked and well mixed. Transfer half of the contents of the pan to a blender, add a little water (if too thick), and blend to a smooth sauce. Add the sauce back to contents of the pan, and season with salt & pepper. Mix well. Optionally, if you're in a mood to indulge, add a little butter or heavy cream to flavor and thicken the sauce. When the koftas are done, remove them from oven, and add them back to the pan. Simmer on low-heat for about 10 minutes to allow the flavors in the pot to mix together. Sprinkle with chopped cilantro leaves.

Serving
Family style: As with most Indian dishes, Chicken Kofta goes well with steamed rice or pulao with a side of fat-free yogurt. It also goes well with Naans or Chappatis.

tandoori chicken

Time = Overnight + 30m (M)

Ingredients
3 lbs assorted chicken pieces, skinned
½ tbsp extra virgin olive oil or lowfat butter
½ cup nonfat plain yogurt
3 large cloves of garlic, finely chopped
1 inch piece of ginger, finely chopped
1 green chili, finely chopped
½ lime, fresh squeezed
1 tsp tandoori masala (if available)
1 tsp chili powder
2 tsp garam masala
Salt and pepper, to taste
2 tbsp red food coloring

Cookware
Large baking tray/sheet (ovenproof to 500+ ºF), nonstick

Prep
Start by skinning the chicken pieces and trimming them of fat and "silver skin". Score the pieces at various points, pour the limejuice over and set aside for 15 minutes. While the chicken pieces are soaking in the limejuice, start the marinade with the chopped garlic and ginger. Add the tandoori masala, garam masala, chili powder, green chili, salt, pepper and food coloring. Add ½ tbsp of olive oil and mix using a blender to create a spicy paste. Add the chicken pieces to the marinade and coat

completely, making sure the marinate gets into all those crevices. Set aside in the refrigerator for 24 hours.

Method
Begin by preheating the oven close to the maximum allowable temperature, 525 ºF. Oil the large baking tray with the remaining ½ tbsp of olive oil. Remove the chicken from the refrigerator and set on the baking tray. Place the tray under the hottest part of the oven (top rack, center). Bake for 25 minutes. Remove the chicken into a separate dish.

Serving
Family style: Arrange the pieces of tandoori chicken on a big serving platter. Garnish with sprigs of cilantro leaves on either side to create a family style serving. Tandoori chicken goes best with Naans or Chappatis.

spicy chicken finger food

Time = 15m + 20m (M)

Ingredients
2 boneless chicken breasts cut in bite-size cubes
2 tbsp extra virgin olive oil
½ red onion, julienne
3 large cloves of garlic, finely chopped
1 inch piece of ginger, finely chopped
¼ habanero pepper, finely chopped
¼ green bell pepper, julienne
¼ red bell pepper, julienne
¼ yellow bell pepper, julienne
½ lime, fresh squeezed
1 tsp chili powder
1 tsp garam masala
1 small cinnamon stick
1 tsp cumin seeds
1 roma tomato, cut lengthwise
Salt and pepper, to taste
Tabasco sauce for a kick
Chopped cilantro

Optional

1 tbsp grated-coconut

2 tbsp honey

Cookware

12" sauté pan, nonstick

Prep

Start by trimming the chicken breasts of fat and "silver skin". Cut the breasts into several bite-size cubes and set aside. Start the marinade with most of the chopped garlic and ginger. Then add the meat masala, garam masala, chili powder, turmeric powder, salt, fresh squeezed limejuice, cinnamon stick and half the cumin seeds. Add a tbsp of olive oil and some cilantro leaves. Mix well to create a spicy mixture. Now add the chicken and coat completely. Set aside in the refrigerator for 3-5 hours.

Method

Heat ½ tbsp olive oil in the sauté pan. Add the marinated chicken and fry until all the pieces are evenly browned, about 2 minutes. Remove the chicken from the pan into a bowl. To the same pan, add the remaining ½ tbsp of olive oil. Add the remaining ginger and garlic, the onions, all peppers, and the rest of the cumin seeds. Add a pinch of salt and fry until the contents of the pan are a little shiny. Add the chicken back to the pan and fry until the pan dries out. At this point, add the tomatoes and continue cooking. Add a little water if the pan is too dry. Cook until all the water has evaporated. Mix in the grated coconut and cook for 10 more seconds. Sprinkle with cilantro leaves if it suits your fancy and ... Serve immediately!

Serving

Arrange the chicken, with veggies and all, on a big serving platter. Insert party picks into the chicken pieces, making sure you include some of veggies in each bite. Alternatively, just set the picks next to the platter on a plate of their own. I guarantee this dish will receive a lot of attention at your tapas party!

pork w/ broccoli

Ingredients
1 pork tenderloin, trimmed of excess fat
1 head of broccoli, washed and separated into flowerets
2 tbsp extra virgin olive oil, for the sauté pan
1 tsp sesame oil, for flavor
1 tsp soy sauce
½ lime, juiced by squeezing
½ onion, thinly sliced
2 cloves of fresh garlic, finely chopped
½ inch piece of fresh ginger, finely chopped
½ red bell pepper, diced
Red chili flakes to taste
Salt and pepper to taste
Chopped cilantro leaves
Chopped basil leaves

Optional
Substitute sesame oil with 1 tsp your favorite curry powder

Cookware
12" sauté pan, nonstick
OR Wok, nonstick

Prep
Cut the pork tenderloin lengthwise and width-wise into bite-size strips. Cut the broccoli into flowerets and wash thoroughly. In a bowl, mix together sesame oil, limejuice, some cilantro leaves, curry powder, dash of soy sauce, chili flakes, salt and pepper. Add the pork pieces and coat very well. Set aside for at least 15 minutes.

Method
Heat the olive oil in a sauté pan. Add the onions, garlic & ginger. Add a pinch of salt to help the cooking. After 15 seconds or so, add the peppers, toss and cook for another 30 seconds. When the onions & peppers get a shiny color, add pork pieces. If the pan dries out, add a

little water. Cook until the pork is almost done. Now add the broccoli and cook for an additional 3-5 minutes until the broccoli takes on a deep green color. Sprinkle with some of the cilantro and basil leaves, toss to mix thoroughly and let rest for a few minutes.

Serving
This dish goes with steamed Jasmine rice.

salmon filet

Time = 3m + 10m (E)

Ingredients
½ lb salmon filet, skin-on one side
½ tbsp extra virgin olive oil or lowfat butter
Few drops of freshly squeezed lemon juice
Salt and pepper, to taste

Cookware
12" skillet, nonstick

Prep
Remove any visible bones from the filet. Squeeze fresh lemon juice over the filet and season with salt & pepper. Let it sit for 5 minutes.

Method
Heat the olive oil (or low-fat butter) in the skillet. Add the salmon filet skin side down. This will prevent the filet from buckling during cooking. Keep an eye on the filet as it cooks. Looking along the thickness of the filet, you should see the skin turning opaque as the salmon cooks. Wait until the opacity reaches half the way up the thickness. At this point, turn the filet over, and wait until the filet becomes opaque evenly across the thickness. Cover, turn down the heat, and let it steam for a few minutes.

Serving
Sprinkle the filet with some more pepper on top. Serve on a clean plate with a fork.

salmon dill toast

Ingredients
1 lb salmon filet, skin-on one side
½ tbsp extra virgin olive oil or lowfat butter
Few drops of freshly squeezed lemon juice
Salt and pepper, to taste
Sprigs of fresh Dill, chopped
Slices of Baguette (French bread)

Cookware
12" skillet, nonstick

Prep
Remove any visible bones from the filet. Squeeze fresh lemon juice over the filet and season with salt & pepper. Let it sit for 5 minutes.

Method
Heat the olive oil (or low-fat butter) in the skillet. Add the salmon filet skin side down. This will prevent the filet from buckling during cooking. Keep an eye on the filet as it cooks. Looking along the thickness of the filet, you should see the skin turning opaque as the salmon cooks. Wait until the opacity reaches half the way up the thickness. At this point, turn the filet over, and wait until the filet becomes opaque evenly across the thickness. Cover, turn down the heat, and let it steam for a few minutes. Remove the flesh from the skin by flaking the filet with a fork. Transfer the flesh back to the skillet and add the chopped dill. Season with salt & pepper if necessary, and combine & cook for 30 seconds.

Serving
Transfer the salmon and dill into the middle of a family style serving platter. Toast the baguette slices as preferred, and arrange around the salmon. Serve with low-fat butter on the side (optional).

WRAPS

In this section, I've included a few recipes for converting leftover curries and sauces into quick, easy and delicious wraps.

Recipe	Time	Difficulty
• Crunchy Chicken Wrap	15m + 3m	Easy
• Chicken & Rice Wrap	5m + 3m	Easy
• Mushroom & Bean Wrap	5m + 3m	Easy

crunchy chicken wrap

Ingredients

  1 flour tortilla, heated
  1 chicken breast, sliced lengthwise into strips
  2 cloves of garlic, finely chopped
  2 tsp of your favorite seasoning
  1 tsp red chili flakes
  ¼ cup all purpose flour
  Tomato slices
  Limejuice to taste
  Salt and pepper, to taste
  Chopped cilantro or parsley
  Crispy lettuce leaves
  Shredded mozzarella

Cookware

  12" sauté pan, nonstick

Prep

Start by slicing the chicken breast lengthwise into strips. Chop the garlic and transfer to a bowl to start the marinade. Add the seasoning, chili flakes, chopped herbs, limejuice and salt & pepper to taste. Mix thoroughly. Now add the chicken and rub with the dry spice mixture. Dump the ¼ cup of all-purpose flour on a flat board and roll the chicken strips in the flour so they get evenly coated. Shake off the extra flour and transfer the strips to a clean plate.

Method

Heat ½ tbsp olive oil in the sauté pan. Add the chicken strips and evenly brown on both sides (about 30 seconds on each side). Turn the heat to medium and cook for about 10 minutes or until the chicken is cooked all the way through (no longer pink on the inside). Remove the chicken onto a plate. Heat a flour tortilla (both sides) on the pan until pliable. Start the wrap by laying the tortilla on a flat board. Smear the tortilla with mayonnaise or your favorite sauce (a tomato red pepper sauce goes really well with this wrap). Add a crispy lettuce leaf and smear with more sauce. Then add two chicken strips and some tomato slices. Roll the ingredients together like a wrap.

Serving
Slice the wrap in half at an angle. Rest the two halves of the wrap on each other on the plate, with the cut ends on the same side. Drizzle with more of your favorite sauce. For a low-carb treatment, eliminate the tortilla altogether by wrapping the ingredients in the lettuce leaf alone. Enjoy!

chicken & rice wrap

Time = 5m + 3m (E)

Ingredients
1 flour tortilla, heated
Leftover chicken curry/sauce
Leftover cooked rice
1 tsp red chili flakes
Limejuice to taste
Salt and pepper, to taste
Chopped cilantro or parsley
Crispy lettuce leaves, shredded
Shredded mozzarella

Cookware
12" sauté pan, nonstick

Prep
Reheat the leftover chicken and rice. Shred the lettuce leaves.

Method
Heat a flour tortilla (both sides) on the pan until pliable. Start the wrap by laying the tortilla on a flat board. Add a few tablespoons of rice and the chicken. Sprinkle with cheese, lettuce and the herbs. Roll the ingredients together like a burrito.

Serving
Serve the burrito whole on the plate with a side of your favorite chips and salsa.

mushroom & bean wrap

Time = 5m + 3m (E)

To make a mushroom & bean wrap, follow the preceding recipe substituting the chicken curry with leftover "mushroom & red kidney beans" (recipe presented earlier). In fact, use this recipe to create wrap with any other leftover sauces or curries.

SOUPS & STEWS

There is perhaps nothing more comforting than a warm soup when you have a runny nose, sore throat, cough or flu. The recipes presented here draw inspiration from Indian and American cuisines and succeed in providing meals that are just a bit different from the usual.

Recipe	Time	Difficulty
• Chicken soup	15m + 30m	Medium
• Spicy chili	20m + 2h	Difficult
• Sambar	15m + 1h	Difficult
• Rasam	10m + 40m	Medium
• Dal fry	10m + 45m	Difficult

chicken soup

Ingredients
6 chicken drumsticks
2 cups low sodium chicken broth
2 tbsp extra virgin olive oil
1 white onion, diced
1 celery stick, diced
2 carrots, diced
3 large cloves of garlic, finely chopped
½ lime, fresh squeezed
2 tsp chili powder
1 tsp of your favorite spice/seasoning
1 (14.5 oz) can diced tomatoes
½ (6 oz) can tomato paste
Salt and pepper, to taste
Chopped cilantro (5 sprigs)
2 tsp Mexican oregano (dried leaves)

Cookware
5 qt stockpot, nonstick (preferred)

Prep
Begin by creating a dry rub with the salt, chili powder, curry powder or
your favorite other spice and cumin. Skin the drumsticks and coat
completely with the rub. Set the drumsticks aside for 10 minutes. Next,
chop the onions, celery, carrots, garlic and ginger.

Method
Heat a tablespoon of olive oil in the stockpot. Add the chicken
drumsticks to the pan and brown on all sides. Remove the chicken into a
bowl. Add the remaining tablespoon of olive oil to the stockpot. Add the
onions, garlic, ginger, celery, carrot. Sprinkle with a little salt and pepper
and let sit for 30 seconds before adding the oregano leaves. Cook until
the vegetables turn shiny and translucent. Add the cans of tomato paste
& diced tomatoes and chili powder and stir.

Now add the browned chicken, mix well with the contents of the pot and let sit for a couple of minutes. Now add the chicken stock or water, more salt and rest of the oregano leaves. Turn the heat to medium-low, cover and cook for 30 minutes, stirring the pot occasionally. Depending on how you like your soup, you may want to add more water or stock at this point if it is too thick. Check to see if the carrots are soft, and the chicken is completely cooked (the chicken meat should easily come apart and no longer pink on the inside). If the soup is not at this stage, cook until you get these results. At this point, remove the drumsticks from the pot and pull all the meat away from the bones. Chop up the meat to desired size pieces and add back to the pot (discard the bones). When the soup comes back to a boil, taste the soup to adjust seasoning, sprinkle with the remaining cilantro on top and let the soup rest, covered, for at least 10 minutes.

Serving
Reheat the soup on the stove when ready to serve. This soup is especially comforting if you're down with a cold, cough or sore throat. The soup is great served by itself or when ladled over steamed rice. Enjoy!

spicy chili

Time = 20m + 2h (D)

Ingredients
1 ½ lb leanest (9% fat) ground beef
1 lb stew meat (beef)
2 (14.5 oz) cans dark red kidney beans
2 cups low sodium beef broth
2 tbsp extra virgin olive oil
1 yellow onion, diced
1 celery stick, diced
2 carrots, diced
½ green pepper, diced
½ red pepper, diced
3 large cloves of garlic, finely chopped
1 ½ habanero peppers, diced
½ lime, fresh squeezed

2 tsp chili powder
1 (14.5 oz) can diced tomatoes
1 (6 oz) can tomato paste
Salt and pepper, to taste
Chopped cilantro (10 sprigs)
Chopped Oregano (6 leaves) –or- dried Mexican oregano (2 tsps)
1 tbsp Tabasco sauce

Cookware
5 qt stockpot, nonstick (preferred)

Prep
Chop the onions, celery, carrots, garlic, ginger and habaneros.

Method
Begin by heating a tablespoon of olive oil in the stockpot. Add the stew
meat to the pan and brown on all sides. Remove the meat into a bowl.
Now add the ground beef into the pan and brown for 2 minutes. Remove
into the bowl with the stew meat.

Add the remaining tablespoon of olive oil to the stockpot. Add the
onions, garlic, celery, carrot and one of the habanero peppers (diced).
Sprinkle with a little salt and pepper and let sit for 30 seconds before
adding the green & red peppers. Stir the ingredients and let cook for
another 30 seconds, before adding half of the chopped oregano leaves.
Cook until the vegetables turn shiny and translucent. Add the cans of
tomato paste & diced tomatoes and chili powder and stir.

Now add the browned meat (stew and ground), mix well with the
contents of the pot and let sit for a couple of minutes. Now add the beef
stock, more water if the chili is too thick, a third of the cilantro leaves,
more salt and rest of the oregano leaves. Turn the heat to medium-low,
cover and cook for 1 hour, stirring the pot occasionally. After an hour
has passed, add the kidney beans, ½ habanero pepper (diced),
limejuice and most of the cilantro (reserving a little for garnish).
Depending on how you like your chili, you may want to add more water
or stock at this point if it is too thick. Cover and cook for 40 minutes.

Check to see if the carrots are soft, and the meat is cooked (the stew meat should easily come apart and no longer pink on the inside). If the chili is not at this stage, cook until you get these results. At this point, taste the chili and mix in the Tabasco for a tangy kick! Sprinkle with the remaining cilantro on top and let the chili rest, covered, for at least ½ hour.

Serving
This chili will taste best when it's allowed to rest for a few hours (preferably overnight). When ready to serve, reheat chili in the microwave or over the stove. Chili is delicious when ladled over steamed rice or by itself with grated cheese on top. This is the perfect dish for any party, especially during those cold winter months. Enjoy!

sambar (Indian lentil soup)

Time = 15m + 1h (D)

Ingredients
2 tbsp vegetable oil
½ tsp mustard seeds
1 onion, chopped into chunks
1 green pepper, chopped into chunks
2 white Yukon potatoes, chopped into chunks
½ lb string beans, trimmed and cut Into halves or thirds
1 cup of Toor Dal (lentils) rinsed and cleaned thoroughly
1 tbsp tamarind paste
A pinch of Asafetida powder (Hing)
1 tsp turmeric powder
1 ½ tbsp sambar powder
1 tsp chili powder
Salt to taste
6 curry leaves

Optional
2 tsp grated coconut
A handful of peanuts

Cookware
5 qt saucepan, nonstick
3 qt saucepan, nonstick

Method
Use the larger saucepan for the lentils. Put the lentils in, cover with twice the volume of water and add the turmeric powder. Cover and cook at low heat until the lentils come close to becoming soft. You might need to add more water. A pressure cooker takes much less time to get the lentils soft. In the smaller saucepan, bring some water to a boil. Poke the potato chunks with a fork, and drop them in the boiling water and reduce the heat. Add a pinch of salt. Cook on low heat until the potatoes are cooked a little more than half the way through. Remove the potatoes and reserve the water from the pan. Clean the saucepan. Heat the oil in the smaller saucepan and add the onions, the peppers, the string beans, the curry leaves and the mustard seeds. Add a pinch of salt and sauté till the ingredients are half-cooked and develop a shine. Now toss in the half-cooked potatoes. Add all the half-cooked veggies and the water reserved from boiling the potatoes to the large saucepan with the lentils. Now add the tamarind paste, asafetida and sambar powder. Mix well and cook on low heat until all the veggies are cooked. Mix in the peanuts and grated coconut. Let the sambar rest for 20 minutes before serving.

Serving
Ladle the sambar over steamed rice. Or eat it with chapattis.

rasam (Indian tomato & lentil soup)

Time = 10m + 40m (M)

Ingredients
2 tbsp vegetable oil
½ tsp mustard seeds
3 big ripe tomatoes
1 cup of Toor Dal (lentils) rinsed and cleaned thoroughly
1 tbsp tamarind paste
A pinch of Asafetida powder (Hing)
1 ½ tbsp rasam powder
Salt to taste

6 curry leaves
Chopped cilantro leaves

Optional
2 tsp grated coconut

Cookware
5 qt saucepan, nonstick
3 qt saucepan, nonstick

Method
Use the larger saucepan for the lentils. Put the lentils in, cover with twice
the volume of water and add the turmeric powder. Cover and cook at low
heat until the lentils come close to becoming soft. You might need to add
more water. A pressure cooker takes much less time to get the lentils
soft. Squish the tomatoes. Heat the oil in the smaller saucepan and
when hot, add the mustard seeds, curry leaves and the squished
tomatoes. Add a pinch of salt and sauté till the ingredients are half-
cooked and develop a shine. Add all the sautéed tomatoes to the larger
saucepan with the lentils. Add twice the volume of water needed to
cover. Now add the tamarind paste, asafetida and rasam powder. Mix
well and cook on low heat until the lentils are completely soft and the
rasam has an even consistency. Add chopped cilantro leaves and grated
coconut. Let the rasam rest for 20 minutes before serving.

Serving
Ladle the rasam over steamed rice for an entrée. Rasam is also
excellent as soup for a first course.

dal fry (Indian lentil soup)

Time = 10m + 45m (D)

Ingredients
2 tbsp vegetable oil
½ tsp mustard seeds
½ red onion, thinly sliced
½ red pepper, sliced into chunks
½ green pepper, sliced into chunks

1 Serrano chili, chopped
2 roma tomatoes
½ cup of Moong Dal (lentils) rinsed and cleaned thoroughly
½ cup of Toor Dal (lentils) rinsed and cleaned thoroughly
1 tbsp tamarind paste
1 tsp chili powder
1 tsp turmeric powder
1 tsp garam masala
1 tsp meat masala
Salt to taste
Chopped oregano leaves (or 1 tsp of powdered oregano)
Chopped cilantro leaves

Optional
2 tsp grated coconut
Use habanero instead of serrano if you like it extra spicy

Cookware
3 qt saucepan, nonstick (OR pressure cooker)
12" covered sauté pan, nonstick (OR a bigger saucepan)

Method
Use the saucepan for the lentils. Put the lentils in, cover with twice the volume of water and add half of the turmeric powder. Cover and cook at low heat until the lentils come close to becoming soft. You might need to add more water. In the sauté pan, heat the olive oil and add the onions, peppers, chilies and salt. When the onions and peppers develop a shine, add the turmeric and chili powder. Add lentils to the sauté pan and continue to fry. Add a little more oil if necessary. Now add the tamarind paste, the tomatoes, the garam masala and meat masala. Add more water for desired consistency. Mix well and cook on low heat until the lentils are completely soft. Add chopped cilantro leaves and grated coconut. Let the dal rest for 20 minutes before serving.

Serving
Ladle the dal over steamed rice for an entrée. Or serve dal as soup with a dollop of plain fat-free yogurt and a sprinkling of fresh chopped cilantro.

RICE, NOODLES & PASTA

Some of the recipes that follow are "one-pot" dishes and as such include vegetables, meat and some form of carbohydrates (rice, noodles or pasta) all in the same dish. For pasta dishes, a second pot is necessary to cook the pasta first.

Recipe	Time	Difficulty
• Steamed basmati rice	5m + 20m	Easy
• Fried rice	10m + 10m	Easy
• Quick-fix pulao	10m + 10m	Easy
• Chicken pulao	15m + 35m	Difficult
• Chicken yakisoba	15m + 25m	Medium
• Fettuccine w/ shrimp, mushrooms & basil	10m + 25m	Medium
• Linguine w/ chicken & parsley	15m + 25m	Medium
• Spaghetti in meat sauce	10m + 30m	Medium

steamed basmati rice

Time = 5m + 20m (E)

Ingredients
2 cups basmati rice, thoroughly washed
3 cups clear, filtered cold water
1 tsp extra virgin olive oil
Salt to taste

Cookware
Casserole dish

Method
Combine the rice, water, salt & oil in the casserole dish and stir well.
Microwave on high for 10 minutes. Microwave on defrost for 10 minutes.

Serving
Fluff gently with a fork and serve immediately.

fried rice

Time = 10m + 10m (E)

Ingredients
1 cup leftover rice (cooked)
2 tsp extra virgin olive oil
1 tsp sesame oil
1 clove of garlic, crushed & chopped
¼ inch piece of ginger, chopped
½ red onion, julienne
¼ green pepper, julienne
¼ red pepper, julienne
½ zucchini, half lengthwise and thinly chopped
4-5 assorted mushrooms, chopped
Handful of bean sprouts
Few splashes of low-sodium soy-sauce
Salt and Pepper to taste
Chopped cilantro leaves

Optional
1 egg (or substitute), beaten
A handful of nuts (peanuts, cashews, or your favorite)

Cookware
11" Wok

Method
Heat the olive oil in the wok. Add the onions, garlic, ginger and a pinch of salt or pepper. Stir-fry for a few seconds before adding the peppers. Continue to stir-fry for a few seconds. Now add the zucchini, mushrooms & bean sprouts. Season with salt and pepper and stir-fry for a few minutes. Add the beaten egg and stir-fry until the egg is scrambled and set. Now add the handful of nuts. Stir-fry and cook until the peanuts are well mixed-in with the other ingredients. Add the cup of leftover cooked rice, a few splashes of soy sauce, the sesame oil, salt and pepper, and stir-fry for a few minutes. Sprinkle with chopped cilantro.

Serving
Transfer the steaming hot fried rice onto a plate. Serve with wedges of lime.

quick-fix pulao (leftover Indian curry & rice)

Time = 10m + 10m (E)

Ingredients
Leftover Indian curry
Leftover rice
Handful of green peas
2 tsp extra virgin olive oil
1 clove of garlic, crushed & chopped
¼ inch piece of ginger, chopped
½ red onion julienne
¼ green pepper, julienne
¼ red pepper, julienne
Salt and Pepper to taste
Chopped cilantro leaves

Optional
1 tsp of your favorite spice

Cookware
11" Wok

Method
Heat the olive oil in the wok. Add the onions, garlic, ginger and a pinch of salt or pepper. Sauté for a few seconds before adding the peppers, and then add the green peas. Season with salt and pepper and cook for a few minutes until the peas are almost done. After 30 seconds, add the leftover curry to the wok. Mix all the ingredients and continue to cook for about a minute. This should warm up the curry (if previously refrigerated). Now add the leftover rice and season with salt, pepper and any additional seasoning. Mix well. Sprinkle with chopped cilantro and stir.

Serving
Transfer the steaming hot curry pulao onto a plate. Serve with wedges of lime.

chicken pulao (one-pot w/ rice, chicken & veggies)

Time = 15m + 35m (D)

Ingredients
2 boneless skinless chicken thighs, chopped into bite-size pieces
3 tsp extra virgin olive oil
2 cloves of garlic, crushed & chopped
¼ inch piece of ginger, chopped
½ red onion, julienne
¼ green pepper, julienne
3 tbsp tomato paste
½ lb green beans, trimmed and halved along the diagonal
1 carrot, julienne (left a little thicker than usual)
Handful of frozen green peas
1 bay leaf
1 cup of basmati rice, thoroughly washed
1½ cups of water (or chicken stock)

½ cup of milk
2 tsp garam masala
1 tsp chili powder
½ tsp turmeric powder
2 tsp red pepper flakes
A pinch of saffron strands
Salt and Pepper to taste
Chopped cilantro leaves
Handful of split cashew nuts

Cookware
12" sauté pan

Prep
Trim the chicken pieces of any fat or silver skin. Cut into bite-size pieces and sprinkle salt, pepper, chili powder and half of the garam masala. Chop the onions, peppers, garlic, ginger, green beans and cilantro. Wash the basmati rice in several changes of water.

Method
Heat the olive oil in the wok. Add chicken pieces to brown on all sides. Remove the chicken into a separate bowl. Now add more oil to the sauté pan if necessary and add the onions, garlic, ginger, peppers, bay leaf and a pinch of salt or pepper. Sauté for a minute and then add the tomato paste. Next, add the remaining spices, salt, pepper, water (or chicken stock) and turn the heat to medium. After about a minute, add the chicken pieces back to the pan. Cook for a minute or so and then add the green beans. Season with salt and pepper, coat the green beans completely with the tomato mixture and cook for a few minutes until the beans are about half done. Next, add the washed basmati rice, more salt and pepper (and more garam masala if necessary) and sauté the raw rice with the pan mixture for about 30 seconds. Then, add 1 cup of water (or chicken stock) and ½ cup of milk, a few drops of oil to keep the rice grains from sticking to each other and the saffron strands. Mix well, cover and turn the heat down to low-medium. Let the rice cook for 15-20 minutes. When the rice is done, sprinkle with cashews and chopped cilantro.

Serving
Pulao is best enjoyed when it is hot. Transfer a portion on a clean plate with an extra sprinkling of cashews if necessary. Serve with your favorite Indian beer.

chicken yakisoba

Time = 15m + 25m (M)

Ingredients
One small packet of pre-cooked yakisoba noodles
2 tsp extra virgin olive oil
¼ red onion, finely chopped
¼ green pepper, julienne
¼ red pepper, julienne
¼ yellow pepper, julienne
3 cloves of garlic, finely chopped
½ inch piece of ginger, finely chopped
2 boneless skinless chicken thighs, sliced in bite-size strips
2 tbsp tomato paste
1 tsp chili powder
1 tsp of your favorite Asian seasoning
¼ head small green cabbage, thinly chopped
1 tsp sesame oil
2 tbsp low-sodium soy sauce
1 tsp hoi sin sauce
1 tbsp red pepper flakes
Salt and pepper, to taste
Chopped cilantro

Cookware
11" Wok

Prep
Trim the chicken pieces of any fat or silver skin. Cut into bite-size pieces and sprinkle salt, pepper, chili powder and your favorite seasoning. Chop the onions, peppers, garlic, ginger, mushrooms, cabbage and cilantro.

Method

Heat the olive oil in the wok. When the oil is hot, add the onions, garlic, ginger and peppers. Season with salt and pepper and cook for 30 seconds until the onions become transparent. Then, add the chicken pieces and cook for about a minute. Next, add half of the soy sauce, half of the sesame oil, hoi sin, the seasonings, chili powder, a little water, and mix well. Turn the heat down to medium and let cook for about 10-15 minutes or until the chicken is completely done (not pink on the inside). Now add the cabbage to the wok, and cook for a few minutes before adding the yakisoba noodles. Sprinkle with salt, pepper, red chili flakes, cilantro, the remaining soy sauce and sesame oil. Add a few drops of olive oil to keep the noodles from sticking and mix well. Continue to cook on high heat for about a minute, tossing the contents of the wok vigorously.

Serving

Transfer a portion of the yakisoba onto a pasta bowl. Sprinkle more cilantro on top if necessary. Serve with your favorite ice-cold beer.

fettuccine w/ shrimp, mushroom & basil

Time = 10m + 25m (M)

Ingredients

Fistful of dried fettuccine pasta
2 tsp extra virgin olive oil
¼ red onion, diced
¼ green pepper, diced
3 cloves of garlic, roughly chopped
6 shitake mushrooms, trimmed and sliced lengthwise
12 jumbo shrimp, peeled and de-veined
2 tbsp tomato paste
1 tsp chili powder
1 tsp of your favorite Italian seasoning
1 tbsp red pepper flakes
Salt & pepper to taste
5 basil leaves, chopped in chiffonade style (long strips)
Grated parmesan cheese to taste

Cookware
12" sauté pan
5 qt sauce pan

Prep
Begin by filling the 5 qt sauce pan with water up to half of its height, and place on high heat. While the water is heating, carefully peel and de-vein the shrimp. Set aside in a bowl and add the Italian seasoning, salt, pepper and some red pepper flakes. Next, chop the onions, green peppers, garlic, mushrooms and basil. Grate the parmesan cheese (if you do not have pre-grated cheese).

Method
When the water comes to a rolling boil, sprinkle a little salt and add the fistful of fettuccine pasta to the pot. As the pasta cooks, heat the olive oil in the sauté pan. When the oil is hot, add the onions, garlic and peppers. Season with salt and pepper and cook for 30 seconds until the onions become transparent. Then, add the tomato paste, the seasonings, chili powder, a little water, and mix well. Turn the heat down to medium and let cook for a few minutes. When the flavor base has come together, add the shrimp, coat evenly in the mixture, cover, and let cook for 4 minutes. Then, add the sliced mushrooms, half of the basil leaves and mix well. Cook for about 8-10 minutes. Keep a constant eye on the pasta while the shrimp cooks (it should be done by now). Drain the pasta and add it to the sauté pan. Sprinkle the pasta with salt, pepper, red chili flakes and the remaining basil leaves. Add a few drops of olive oil to keep the pasta from sticking and mix well with the shrimp and mushroom sauce. Turn the heat to low, cover and cook for about 2 minutes. Now sprinkle the grated parmesan over the pasta, cover and let rest for 2 minutes until the cheese melts.

Serving
Transfer a portion of the pasta onto a pasta bowl. Grate more cheese and more chopped basil on top if necessary. Serve with Italian bread and your favorite chardonnay.

linguine w/ chicken & parsley

Ingredients
Fistful of dried linguine pasta
2 tsp extra virgin olive oil
¼ red onion, diced
¼ green pepper, diced
3 cloves of garlic, roughly chopped
2 boneless skinless chicken thighs, sliced in bite-size strips
2 tbsp tomato paste
1 tsp creole mustard
1 tsp chili powder
1 tsp of your favorite Italian seasoning
1 tbsp red pepper flakes
Salt & pepper to taste
5 parsley sprigs, de-stemmed and chopped finely
Grated parmesan cheese to taste

Cookware
12" sauté pan
5 qt sauce pan

Prep
Begin by filling the 5 qt sauce pan with water up to half of Its height, and place on high heat. While the water is heating, cut the chicken thighs into bite-size strips. Set aside in a bowl and add the Italian seasoning, salt, pepper and some red pepper flakes. Next, chop the onions, green peppers, garlic, mushrooms and parsley. Grate the parmesan cheese (if you do not have pre-grated cheese).

Method
When the water comes to a rolling boil, sprinkle a little salt and add the fistful of linguine pasta to the pot. As the pasta cooks, heat the olive oil in the sauté pan. When the oil is hot, add the onions, garlic and peppers. Season with salt and pepper and cook for 30 seconds until the onions become transparent. Then, add the chicken pieces and cook for about a minute. Next, add the tomato paste, the seasonings, chili powder, a little water, and mix well. Turn the heat down to medium and let cook for

about 10-15 minutes or until the chicken is completely done (not pink on the inside). The linguine should have been cooked by now. Drain the pasta and add it to the sauté pan. Sprinkle the pasta with salt, pepper, red chili flakes and parsley. Add a few drops of olive oil to keep the pasta from sticking and mix well with the chicken and tomato sauce. Turn the heat to low, cover and cook for about 2 minutes. Now sprinkle the grated parmesan over the pasta, cover and let rest for 2 minutes until the cheese melts.

Serving
Transfer a portion of the pasta onto a pasta bowl. Grate more cheese and chopped parsley on top if necessary. Serve with Italian bread and your favorite merlot.

spaghetti in meat sauce

Time = 10m + 30m (M)

Ingredients
Fistful of dried spaghetti pasta
2 tbsp extra virgin olive oil
¼ red onion, diced
¼ green pepper, diced
3 cloves of garlic, roughly chopped
1 lb leanest ground beef (9% or less fat)
2 tbsp tomato paste
1 tsp chili powder
1 tsp of your favorite Italian seasoning
1 tbsp red pepper flakes
Salt & pepper to taste
5 parsley sprigs, de-stemmed and chopped finely
Grated parmesan cheese to taste

Cookware
12" sauté pan
5 qt sauce pan

Prep
Begin by filling the 5 qt sauce pan with water up to half of its height, and place on high heat. While the water is heating, chop the onions, green peppers, garlic, mushrooms and parsley. Grate the parmesan cheese (if you do not have pre-grated cheese).

Method
When the water comes to a rolling boil, sprinkle a little salt and add the fistful of spaghetti pasta to the pot. As the pasta cooks, heat the olive oil in the sauté pan. When the oil is hot, add the ground beef and keep stirring to break up the meat. When the beef is browned, remove it into a bowl and add the onions, garlic and peppers to the same pan. Season with salt and pepper and cook for 30 seconds until the onions become transparent. Then, add the tomato paste, the seasonings, chili powder, a little water, and mix well. Now add the beef back to the pan, turn the heat down to medium and let cook for about 25-30 minutes or until the beef is done (not pink on the inside). The spaghetti would have finished cooking by now (takes about 10 minutes to cook). Drain the pasta and add it to the sauté pan. Sprinkle the pasta with salt, pepper, red chili flakes and parsley. Add a few drops of olive oil to keep the pasta from sticking and mix well with the meat and tomato sauce. Turn the heat to low, cover and cook for about 2 minutes. Now sprinkle the grated parmesan over the pasta, cover and let rest for 2 minutes until the cheese melts.

Serving
Transfer a portion of the pasta onto a pasta bowl. Grate more cheese and sprinkle more chopped parsley on top if necessary. Serve with Italian bread and your favorite cabernet.

References

1. http://news.bbc.co.uk/1/hi/health/966757.stm. UK Survey: 59% of women surveyed preferred food to sex.

2. http://home3.americanexpress.com/corp/latestnews/everyday.asp. Consumers spend $3700/year on groceries.

3. http://www.businessweek.com/ebiz/9911/el1119.htm. 60% of consumers dislike grocery shopping (dated Nov 19, 1999).

4. http://www.rgj.com/news/stories/html/2002/04/15/12110.php. More than 2/3 of our buying decisions are made after we enter the grocery store

5. http://www.newhomemaker.com/money/smartshop.html. Impulse buying at grocery stores makes up 20%-50% of a typical bill.

Alu: Indian word for Potato.

Bhindi: Indian word for Okra.

Chiffonade: Most commonly refers to a style of chopping basil leaves when the leaves are stacked on top of each other, rolled along the width and cut into strips

Chole: Indian word for chick peas.

Crepe: Wafer-thin pancakes made from a base of eggs, flour and milk. Crepes stands are very common in France.

Diced: Refers to a style of chopping when the vegetable is cut along all three dimensions to yield small square pieces. Cutting vegetables like this retains the body of the vegetable but exposes a lot of surface area for quicker cooking than when vegetables are left in bigger chunks.

Garam masala: A special blend of Indian spices made of peppercorns, cardamom, clove, and many other aromatic spices

Gobi: Indian word for Cauliflower.

Julienne: Refers to a style of cutting when vegetables are cut into thin long strips. Most often used with carrots, peppers and celery for stir-fry.

Kheema: Ground lamb or beef

Kofta: Shaped into balls

Meat masala: Dry Indian spice

Mirepoix: Refers to carrots, celery and onion – a great combination of aromatic vegetables that serve as a foundation for many soups and other dishes

Mutter: Peas

Palak: Spinach

Paneer: Indian cottage cheese

Pulao: Indian style of cooking rice with vegetables and aromatic spices to create a one-pot dish

Rasam: South Indian lentil soup without vegetables

Rasam powder: A special blend of spices that is used in making Rasam. Available in Indian grocery stores.

Saffron: Saffron is most often used in Indian desserts and pulaos. It is most often used with milk to impart a yellowish-orange color and a unique taste that permeates throughout the dish. It is the most expensive spice in the world.

Sambar: South Indian lentil soup with vegetables

Stock: A thin liquid that contains the essential flavor of meats and vegetables – e.g., chicken stock is made from leftover pieces of chicken bones that are sautéd with aromatic vegetables like carrots, celery, onions and herbs and spices like bay leaves, salt, pepper, chili powder, etc. Water is then added and the mixture simmers for about an hour to extract all flavors out of the meat and vegetables. The resulting liquid is strained and used to add body to various dishes.

Toor dal: Indian lentils used in Sambar, Rasam, Dal Fry and several other dishes. Available in Indian grocery stores.

Trinity: A Cajun term for onions, celery and green peppers

Turmeric: Often called the poor man's saffron, this is a yellow colored spice most often used in Indian curries to impart a yellow color to the dish.

Index

114

Why I wrote this book

THANKS FOR READING through my first book! I

hope the chapters in Part I were informative, and the recipes in Part II offered a glimpse at the possibilities that lie in front you in your own kitchen.

I had always been curious about cooking since I was a teenager in India several years ago. That curiosity turned into a hobby when I moved to America for graduate studies in 1996. Many of the benefits I've mentioned in the first chapter of this book were motivations for me to adopt this hobby more seriously. In just a few years after doing so, I lost about 20 pounds in weight, saved a bunch of money and gained new friends. Following graduate school I moved to Seattle where I submitted several recipes to the KCTS Cooks TV series that have been printed in many of their cookbooks.

One of the biggest challenges for me was to find a no-nonsense book that would teach me exactly what I needed to know to start cooking. I found cookbooks that were based on specific cuisines (Italian food), ingredients (pasta recipes), meal courses (appetizers) and every other combination under the sun, but absolutely none that would teach me just what I needed. I'm referring to the actual mechanics of cooking for someone who has never done this before, and the much needed help in setting up a basic functional kitchen and shopping for groceries. The beginner books that I did find ran 500+ pages and were full of information that I didn't need and came at a price that I didn't want to spend. Further, as I mentioned before, most beginner books only touched upon activities inside the kitchen and mentioned nothing about how to set up a functional kitchen or how to shop for groceries – things I had little experience with.

Given the many benefits that I have directly experienced from cooking and my frustrations about cookbooks that were available on the market, I decided that I had to write a simple, to-the-point book that would teach novice cooks exactly what they need to know to adopt this king of hobbies. This book starts with a reassuring statement about the plethora of benefits of cooking and offers help inside *and outside* the kitchen. The book also presents a step-by-step approach to cooking that applies to almost any dish (as evidenced by the variety of recipes presented herein). The recipes mention not only the mechanics of cooking, but also the kind of cookware used, the amount of time required and the level of difficulty that each dish represents.

Thanks again for buying my book. As of this writing, I'm now an MBA student in the city of Chicago and continue to cook regularly. If you have any questions or comments about this book, or want to share a new recipe, please email me directly at the address provided below. I will be very glad to hear from you!

Vin

Vineeth Subramanyam
EverydayCooking@gmail.com
http://www.vineeths.com/
August 2006

About Vineeth

Vineeth Subramanyam got interested in cooking as a teenager and has been cooking actively for several years. He has submitted recipes to public television shows that have been printed in cookbooks. He has also organized and competed in cook-offs. Vineeth has worked on this book largely in his spare time. This is Vineeth's first book. Vineeth is currently an MBA student at the University of Chicago's Graduate School of Business and lives in Chicago. For more information, visit Vineeth's website at http://www.vineeths.com/

Made in the USA
Lexington, KY
20 December 2009